# DANIEL WEBSTER AND THE POLITICS
## OF AVAILABILITY

# DANIEL WEBSTER

# AND THE POLITICS OF AVAILABILITY

## NORMAN D. BROWN

UNIVERSITY OF GEORGIA PRESS, ATHENS

Library of Congress Catalog Card Number: 68-54089
Standard Book Number: 8203-0231-7

The University of Georgia Press, Athens 30601

The text of this book was set on the Linotype in 11/13 Baskerville
and printed by The Seeman Printery, Inc., Durham, N.C.
Designed by Fred Thompson.

# PREFACE

This book is about the presidential
ambitions of Daniel Webster during the years in which a second
party system of National Republican-Whig and Democratic
parties emerged out of the superficial Republican unity of the
"Era of Good Feelings." The transition from National Republican to Whig between 1832 and 1834 is commonly viewed as the
logical consequence of President Andrew Jackson's war on the
Second Bank of the United States, with the congressional opposition organizing around the issue of executive usurpation. For
example, one historian has recently written, "Although the
anti-Jackson party continued to call itself National Republican
through the campaign of 1832, it abruptly and consciously became proto-Whig with the veto message."* Yet I would argue
that such a thesis ignores the potentially disruptive effect of
the nullification crisis of 1832-1833 on emerging party alignments.
In 1833, Webster was deeply involved in efforts to supplant
Henry Clay as the premier leader of the National Republican
party, so that he could carry its members into a coalition

* Lynn L. Marshall, "The Strange Stillbirth of the Whig Party," *American
Historical Review*, LXXII (1967), 446.

with Jackson on an anti-nullification "Constitution and Union" platform, and thus secure his own election to the presidency in 1836. These efforts failed, but politicians at the time took them seriously, and so must historians. Nullification lost its importance as a national issue, and most political leaders were happy to drop it and turn to other questions. Had it been otherwise, had Webster been able to overcome formidable obstacles and effect an alliance with the President, American party development might have proceeded along ideological lines with nationalists aligned against proponents of state rights.

Thereafter Webster sought the presidency within the Whig fold, and made his major bid in the election of 1836. His supporters, members of the northeastern business aristocracy, presented him to the electorate as a man superbly qualified for the highest office, a "statesman" candidate in the tradition of the presidency before the advent of Jackson. But younger Whig wire-pullers like William H. Seward and the brilliant strategist, Thurlow Weed, realized that the Whigs must copy Jacksonian campaign methods to win the White House. Webster, they concluded, would not do; he had no magnetism and "did not take with the people." Instead they found in the elderly General William H. Harrison of Ohio, the "Hero of Tippecanoe," the Whig counterpart of the all-conquering "Hero of New Orleans." Harrison was taken up because he was, in the political language of the day, the most "available" Whig candidate in the North. The term implied a willingness to accept a man for public office, without much regard to fitness, but solely on the grounds of his supposed popularity with the mass of ordinary voters.

When Webster, representing in this election the older politics of deference, was overwhelmed by Harrison in the fall of 1835 and swept aside as his party's nominee in the North, it was an enduring triumph for the new Whig politics of availability preached by Seward, Weed, and some western leaders. In 1840, 1848, and 1852, the Whigs would pass over Clay or Webster to nominate military heroes for the presidency. And once firmly established, the hero-candidate tradition has remained viable in American politics from Grant to Eisenhower.

I am indebted to my colleagues, Professors H. Wayne Morgan and James Curtis, who read the manuscript and offered many valuable criticisms. Quotations from the Adams Papers are taken from the microfilm edition, by permission of the Massachusetts Historical Society. I wish to thank the Office of the Graduate Dean, the University of Texas at Austin, for a grant-in-aid to prepare the final manuscript.

Norman D. Brown

April 1969
Austin, Texas

TO MY MOTHER AND FATHER

# CONTENTS

# DANIEL WEBSTER AND THE POLITICS
## OF AVAILABILITY

# THE GREATEST OFFICE

**1** In the early summer of 1852, Secretary of State Daniel Webster was traveling in a railroad car with a friend, William Bates. Just a few days before Webster had lost the Whig nomination for President to General Winfield Scott, and the conversation turning to that subject, Bates, to ease the old man's mind, remarked that perhaps the office was, after all, not that important to a man of his great fame. Webster thought for a moment and then said firmly: "To be frank with you Mr. Bates, the same question has occurred to me. And perhaps it is as you say; perhaps I am just as well without that office. But, sir, it is a great office; why, Mr. Bates, it is the greatest office in the world; and I am but a man, sir, I want it, I want it."[1]

Webster's ambition was perfectly normal for a man of his acknowledged stature and talents. Few American statesmen of note have not dreamed of ending their public careers in the White House. Webster's two great rivals, Henry Clay and John C. Calhoun, were as eager (and as unsuccessful) in that quest. Clay and Calhoun were avowed candidates as early as the presidential election of 1824; but Webster, a leader in New England's Federalist party, was not seriously considered for the presidency until the demise of that ill-fated party made possible a new political alignment. Indeed, it was not until after his famous Senate debate with Robert Y. Hayne of South Carolina in January 1830 that he began to be widely mentioned as a worthy candidate for that high office. Rufus Choate, one of Webster's closest friends, attributed his failure to obtain the presidency to this fact. "Mr. Webster has been at least twelve years behind his glory and his country," he told Edward Parker in 1850. "He didn't find out till well advanced that he stood a chance for the Presidency. Meanwhile, he had hit right and left, and made many enemies. He had . . . got a set of cold New England manners, and had thoroughly conformed himself for home consumption."[2]

During his early public career, Webster was a strict constructionist and anti-nationalist, as befitted the spokesman of a Yankee "conscious minority." Elected to the House of Representatives from New Hampshire as a Federalist in 1812, at the age of thirty, he opposed the War of 1812, although he was not willing to go as far as secession. Webster had nothing to do with the Hartford Convention, except to advise Governor John Gilman of New Hampshire against sending delegates, and the state was not officially represented, though two of its counties along the Connecticut River were. He voted against establishing a second national bank chiefly on partisan grounds. As a spokesman for the dominant merchants and shippers of New England, he vigorously opposed the tariffs of 1816 and 1824; and in a speech before a public meeting in Boston, in 1820, he attacked the protective tariff theory so ably that "in after years, as a protectionist, he was hard put to refute himself."[3] But once New England's economic emphasis shifted from commerce to manufacturing, Webster quit the free trade fold and joined manufacturers in urging a protective tariff.

What national reputation Webster enjoyed prior to his debate with Hayne was largely derived from his appearances before the United States Supreme Court. During the period 1819 to 1827, the height of his practice, he joined with Chief Justice John

Marshall in giving a nationalistic, Hamiltonian interpretation to the Constitution. His famous arguments in the *Dartmouth College* case and *McCulloch v. Maryland* (1819) brought him to the front rank of the federal bar. After the death of William Pinkney in 1822, he became firmly established as the nation's leading constitutional lawyer, overshadowing all others in the importance of cases argued and in his mastery of great principles of constitutional law.[4]

Yet, in spite of his prominence as a constitutional lawyer, Webster was not satisfied. He was "as ambitious as Caesar" and "would not be outdone by any man." While walking with William Plumer, the younger, on the Capitol grounds one evening in 1822, Webster passionately confessed his desire for fame. "Nothing, nothing, I have done absolutely nothing!" he exclaimed. "At thirty, Alexander had conquered the world; and I am forty." Plumer reminded him that Julius Caesar at forty had also done nothing. "Ay," replied Webster, "that is better; there is something in that. Caesar at forty had done nothing: we may then say at forty, one may still hope to do great things."[5]

Webster had moved to Boston in 1816, and in 1823 he was again elected to the House of Representatives. During the election of 1824, with Republicans John Quincy Adams, Andrew Jackson, Henry Clay, John C. Calhoun, and William H. Crawford all in the field, Webster stood aloof, expecting the rival candidates to offer explicit assurances that deserving Federalists would be given office under their administration. When the election went into the House, Webster obtained a virtual promise from Adams that he would appoint at least one Federalist and probably others. With this "pledge" in his pocket, Webster dropped his noncommittal stance and worked effectively for Adams among Federalist members from New York and Maryland.[6] There was some talk of Webster as a member of Adams' cabinet; he himself said there was "not a particle of probability of any such offer."[7] Still later it was rumored that Webster would become the American minister in London. But the President noted in his diary: "All the friends of the Administration are agreed that the political effect of the appointment of Mr. Webster would be very unfavorable."[8]

Swallowing his disappointment, Webster remained in the House where his ability in debate made him the administration spokesman. Philip P. Barbour of Virginia, once the speaker of that body, confessed he considered Webster the most powerful man "ever sent from the North."[9] Elected to the Senate in 1827, he led the largest remnant of the surviving Federalists into the National Republican party of Henry Clay and President Adams— a party dedicated to those nationalist principles he had once ardently opposed. But with all his acknowledged talents, it seemed unlikely that he would ever win eminence outside New England, even under a new party banner. John McLean, Postmaster-General under Adams, predicted that "his course in the late war will always prove the grave of his prospects." In the election of 1828, when Adams was defeated for re-election by General Andrew Jackson, who swept the South and West, McLean declared that Webster's prominence in the contest had done "great injury" to the President's cause.[10] Webster himself remarked after the election that it would be many years before New England would give another President to the United States.[11]

No one could deny that Webster looked like a President. He was an extraordinary figure, and at the age of forty, was considered the handsomest man in Congress. He was five feet ten inches in height, strongly built, had a large head, very high forehead, a dark complexion, large black eyes ("like dull anthracite furnaces needing only to be *blown*," remarked historian Thomas Carlyle), jet black hair, very heavy eyebrows, and a mastiff mouth.[12] "To strangers his countenance appeared stern, but when lighted up by conversation, it was bland and agreeable," wrote his private secretary, Charles Lanman. "He was slow and stately in his movements, and his dress was invariably neat and elegant; his favorite suit for many years having been a blue or brown coat, a buff vest, and black pantaloons."[13]

As an orator, Webster clearly outshone all his competitors. When the English traveller, Harriet Martineau, visited the United States Senate in 1835, she was impressed most of all by "the transcendent Webster, with his square forehead and his cavernous eyes":

When he rises, his voice is moderate, and his manner quiet, with the slightest possible mixture of embarrassment; his right hand rests upon his desk, and the left by his side. Before his first head is finished, however, his voice has risen so as to fill the chamber and ring again, and he has fallen into his favorite attitude, with his left hand under his coat-tail, and the right in full action. At this moment, the eye rests upon him as upon one under the true inspiration of seeing the invisible and grasping the impalpable.[14]

Webster had a powerful and logical mind, with remarkable retentive powers. Worshipers called him the "Godlike Daniel." His faults were largely those of temperament. Though never a rich man, he had a taste for ease and luxury. He was inordinately fond of good food and fine clothes, of port and madeira, and constant adulation. To pay his enormous debts, he borrowed (and never repaid) huge sums from the Bank of the United States, and his friends periodically solicited contributions from the "best" people in Boston, so that he could remain in Congress to look after their interests. Hard work over a long period of time was beyond him; he seldom spoke in the Senate, and generally bestirred himself only on some constitutional question, when he could impress his colleagues and the gallery with his knowledge and reasoning powers. At other times, he sat at his desk, writing letters or dreaming, so oblivious to his surroundings that a member of his party had frequently to jog his elbow when his vote was wanted.[15] To the South Carolina Unionist, Benjamin Perry, "Mr. Webster appeared like a great seventy-four gun ship, which required deeper water, larger space, and stronger wind to be set in motion. He required a great occasion to bring forth his great powers."[16] A senator compared him to "the heavy artillery in the army of Napoleon, silencing the batteries of the enemy, as at Austerlitz and Jena."[17]

In January 1830, Webster at last had an opportunity "to do great things." A bitter debate broke out in the Senate over a resolution by Samuel Foote of Connecticut proposing a temporary restriction on the sale of public lands. On January 18 Thomas Hart Benton of Missouri denounced the resolution as another manifestation of eastern hostility to the West; and the next day,

Robert Y. Hayne of South Carolina, seeing an opportunity to link the West with the South in defense of state rights, repeated Benton's charges against the East. He announced that the South would always sympathize with the West, and advocated an alliance between the two sections in opposition to the protective tariff.

Webster was arguing a case in the Supreme Court room below the Senate, and having nothing to do for the moment, walked into the chamber as Hayne was rising to speak. During Hayne's remarks, he listened attentively. "When he sat down," Webster wrote afterward, "my friends said he must be answered, and I thought so too, and being thus got in, thought I must go through . . . ."[18] The next day (January 20), Webster answered Hayne and denied his charge of eastern hostility to the West. In reply, Hayne discussed at length John C. Calhoun's nullification doctrine and argued the right of a sovereign state to declare null and void an unconstitutional federal law. To this Webster, in his "Second Reply to Hayne" (January 26-27, 1830), answered with a powerful defense of national sovereignty. He insisted that the Constitution came not from the states as such but from the American people, that the national government was not merely a creature of the states, and that nullification was a false and futile doctrine destructive of national unity. As those on the floor and in the gallery of the Senate chamber sat enthralled, Webster brought his mighty effort to a close with a magnificent peroration, ending "Liberty *and* Union, now and forever, one and inseparable!"[19]

This peroration, which became a favorite declamation piece with school boys of the coming generation, enshrined in the hearts of the northern and western people a semi-mystical conception of the Union. More immediately, Webster's argument went home to Andrew Jackson in the White House. There is some evidence that the President expected Webster to demolish Hayne.[20] Jackson counted himself a state rights man, and was friendly to Hayne, the brother of his former aide-de-camp and Inspector General; but he never doubted the sovereignty of the nation. At a Jefferson birthday dinner on April 13, 1830, which the nullification party had arranged to enlist the President in their cause, the old soldier, looking straight at Calhoun, gave the toast: "Our Federal Union—it must be preserved!" Webster predicted that "some schism" would grow out of the dinner,[21] and he was not mistaken. He had opened a rift between the West and the South in the Democratic party, which was further widened the next year by a final break between Jackson and Calhoun. A fallen angel, his hopes for the presidency blasted, the embittered South Carolinian now joined those in his state who urged implementation of the nullification doctrine.

The "Second Reply to Hayne" gave Webster a reputation as one of the three or four leading statesmen of the nation. Hundreds of complimentary letters piled up on his desk. Madison, Monroe, and Clay praised his patriotism. "It crushes 'nullification,' wrote Madison, "and must hasten an abandonment of 'secession.' "[22] To meet the public demand, more than one hundred thousand copies of a carefully revised "Reply" in pamphlet form were distributed by the summer of 1831.[23] Of all American statesmen the one "who has succeeded in riveting most strongly the attention of the whole Union, is undoubtedly Mr. Webster," wrote the English traveller, Thomas Hamilton. "From the Gulf of St. Lawrence to that of Mexico, from Cape Sable to Lake Superior, his name has become, as it were, a household word."[24] The Boston merchant prince, Amos Lawrence, told his son that "Mr. Webster never stood so high in this country as at this moment; and I doubt if there be any man, either in Europe or America, his superior." In the fall, Lawrence sent Webster an expensive service of plate, as a testimony of his personal regard.[25]

His new stature as a national statesman made Webster a potential presidential candidate, and his biographers agree that after 1830 the hope of reaching the White House was constantly in the back of his mind.[26] George Ticknor Curtis, Webster's literary executor, noted in his official biography that the years 1830-1831 marked "the period in Mr. Webster's life when he began to be considered . . . the most suitable person to be brought forward as a candidate for the presidency"; and it was "one of the facts which constitute Mr. Webster's justification for allowing himself to be drawn into that long candidacy, in respect to which he was destined to be always unsuccessful, that some of the best and wisest men of his time . . . originally awakened this desire in his breast."[27]

It appeared, however, that Webster must wait until 1836 to run for the presidency. After the defeat of John Quincy Adams in 1828, National Republican leaders accepted Henry Clay of Kentucky as the party's logical candidate to try and unseat Jackson in 1832. Joseph Gales, senior editor of the Washington *National Intelligencer,* told Webster that "of all men . . . I should prefer you to any other for the presidency. I hope in God the time will come which will give to that station 'one Roman more.' " But Clay was so prominently before the people, so identified with western feeling, and so acceptable to the East, that "we must go for him if we go alone. I cannot bear the idea of any other being thought of by those who approve his politics."[28] In May 1830, Webster assured Clay of his hearty support for the nomination. "I think you can not be kept back from the contest," he wrote. "The people will bring you out, *nolens volens.* Let them do it." Toward the close of his letter, he said:

> Parties must now, necessarily, be started out anew; and the great ground of difference will be Tariff and Internal Improvements. You are necessarily at the head of one party, and General Jackson will be, if he is not already, identified with the other. The question will be put to the country. Let the country decide it.[29]

But as the campaign progressed, the cordiality with which Webster had accepted Clay gradually cooled. A perceptible change took place in the New Englander's attitude by the spring of 1831, influenced perhaps by the conviction that Clay could not be elected. It was clear that the Antimasonic party[30] could not be persuaded to endorse Clay, who was a Mason; and Webster, who was not, received assurances from important persons that there was nothing they desired more than to make him President, if he could arrange a union between the National Republicans and Antimasons.[31] As early as the summer of 1830, he received overtures from Antimasonic leaders in western Pennsylvania.[32] The election of the state legislature in Kentucky in August 1831 was viewed across the country as a test of Clay's popularity; and its indecisive result proved that his strength was not as great as had been supposed. The Kentuckian was so disheartened that he thought of abandoning the struggle, but finally decided to re-enter the United States Senate and take direct command of the congressional opposition.

Shortly before this election, the wealthy Salem, Massachusetts merchant, Stephen White, told the National Republican state central committee that Webster's friends would support Clay until defeat in the Kentucky election, "fatal to his success," should call for a new candidate. In such a case, as White informed Webster, "I thought neither yourself nor your friends should be unmindful how prominent your claims were when compared with those of any other individual." According to White, the leaders of all parties whom Webster had met on his travels were well disposed toward him and there was a strong disposition "to create a *constitutional party* and to place you at the head of it. . . ."[33]

Webster wrote Charles Miner, editor of the weekly West Chester *Village Record,* and one of the most influential National Republican journalists in Pennsylvania, that the Kentucky election, while not quite as bad as first reported, was still unsatisfactory, and had produced an unfavorable impression in Massachusetts. He agreed with Miner that there was very little chance of electing Clay; even with the vote of Kentucky, "I do not perceive where we are to find enough others to make a majority." The one chance to save the country from further and worse misrule was to bring forward a man who would unite the Antimasons and National Republicans of New York and Pennsylvania and win the votes of those states. Add Ohio, New England, New Jersey, Delaware, and Maryland, and the opposition would be able to elect a President. But Webster feared that there was very little prospect of finding such a candidate. The Antimasons were intent on pushing John McLean of the United States Supreme Court; but he would never do; "our friends in New England and elsewhere will never be brought to support him. As against him the election of Gen'l Jackson would be certain."

Miner had said that Webster himself possessed a portion of

the confidence of the Antimasons and National Republicans. The Senator replied with becoming modesty:

> Perhaps it may be so, but I cannot think the country is inclined to bring me forward, and it is certain that I shall do nothing to bring myself forward. I have little experience in public affairs, and have not been long enough before the country to produce great general confidence. My only merit is an ardent attachment to the country and the constitution of Government, and I am already more than paid for all my efforts, if you and other good men think I have done any thing to defend the Constitution and promote the welfare of the country. In the favor which those efforts have attracted towards me, I see promise of a real, substantial, fixed attachment among the people to the Constitution. The great body of the community is quite sound on that point. And that is the feeling which we ought to cultivate, and on which we must rely. If we are to bring about a change it will be done by us as a Union party.[34]

Despite this disclaimer, Webster discreetly explored the possibility that he might be called upon to supplant Clay in the canvass. Hiram Ketchum, a National Republican leader in New York City, later testified that prior to the National Republican convention in Baltimore in December 1831, he had "very full and free conversations" with Webster in respect to a nomination. Ketchum stated without qualification that Webster did not favor Clay, "and I know that he desired the nomination for himself." Ketchum was favorable to Webster's selection, then and subseqently, but other National Republican leaders in New York overruled his preference, and he was compelled to say so to Webster. The Senator acquiesced and the convention unanimously nominated Clay for President, with John Sergeant of Pennsylvania as his running mate.[35]

The Antimasonic party had held its national convention in Baltimore on September 26, 1831, and nominated William Wirt, a prominent Maryland lawyer, for the presidency. Webster was asked by Antimasonic leaders to aid in securing Clay's withdrawal before the National Republican convention met, so that the anti-Jackson men could unite behind Wirt. He was told that if Wirt was elected, he could have any place in the cabinet. Webster refused to help. He warned Ambrose Spencer of New York, a delegate to the National Republican convention and a Wirt advocate, that he would find very little support for that gentleman's nomination at Baltimore. He thought Wirt had acted under great misinformation in accepting the Antimasonic nomination.

> I believe Mr. Wirt's nomination has *secured* Genl. Jackson's re-election! I believe he cannot take a vote from Genl. Jackson, but may take a few from Mr. Clay; that is, the Vermont votes; but a greater evil resulting from his nomination is, that it greatly discouraged those, who were desirous of producing a change in the Genl Administration, & greatly encouraged the friends of the present President. I hope, indeed, for a different result, but I do not expect it.[36]

The Second Bank of the United States was the chief issue in the election of 1832. Although its charter did not expire until 1836, the president of the Bank, the able and cultivated Philadelphian Nicholas Biddle, was urged by Webster and Clay to seek a recharter before the election. Webster told Biddle that after Jackson's re-election, "there would be a poor chance for the Bank."[37] When a recharter bill passed Congress in July 1832, Jackson, viewing the institution as undemocratic, unconstitutional, and monopolistic, accepted the challenge and returned the measure with a stinging veto message. Webster, who was retained as a legal adviser by the Bank and was on the board of directors of its Boston branch, led the fight in the Senate with Clay against the President. The veto message, he pontificated, was *"trash* on the constitutional question." But the veto could not be overridden, Congress adjourned, and the question was taken to the people.[38]

The result of the election was never really in doubt. Jackson confidently said to Senator Hill of New Hampshire, "Isaac, it'll be a walk." Old Hickory was enormously popular, and the opposition was split by the inability of the National Republicans and Antimasons to agree on one candidate. Even if the two parties had been united, the outcome would have been the same. As it was, Jackson won a decisive victory. Clay carried only Massachusetts,

Rhode Island, Connecticut, Delaware, and Kentucky, with five votes from Maryland. The Electoral College gave Jackson 219 votes to Clay's 49, Wirt's 7 (Vermont), and John Floyd's 11 (South Carolina). In the popular vote, Jackson had a majority of 124,392 over his opponents.[39] Rufus Choate, National Republican congressman from Massachusett's Essex South district, lamented after the result had been announced: "The news from the voting states blows over us like a great cold storm. I suppose all is lost, and that the map will be rolled up for twelve years to come. Happy if when it is opened again, no state shall be missing."[40]

Clay's overwhelming defeat threw the Kentuckian's career in eclipse, placed Webster in the forefront of the National Republican party, and strengthened his desire to be a presidential candidate in 1836. But Clay's defeat had seriously weakened the party; and without additional popular support, its final extinction was likely. This fact, together with the growing threat to the Union posed by the nullification movement in South Carolina, suggested to Webster the formation of a new party organized in defense of the Constitution and the Union with himself at its head. The plan developed more fully in 1833. Stephen White had informed him of a strong disposition to form such a party as early as 1831; and although all thought of a new organization was abandoned during the campaign of 1832, the idea of a new party had taken firm root in Webster's mind.

## NOTES

*1.* Quoted in Claude M. Fuess, *Daniel Webster* (Boston, 1930), II, 268.

*2.* Edward G. Parker, *Reminiscences of Rufus Choate, The Great American Advocate* (New York, 1860), p. 238.

*3.* Richard N. Current, *Daniel Webster and the Rise of National Conservatism* (Boston, 1955), p. 34.

*4.* Maurice G. Baxter, *Daniel Webster & the Supreme Court* (Amherst, 1966).

*5.* William Plumer, "Reminiscences of Daniel Webster," James W. McIntyre (ed.), *The Writings and Speeches of Daniel Webster* (Boston, 1903), XVII, 560. (Hereafter cited as *Writings and Speeches.*)

*6.* Shaw Livermore, Jr., *The Twilight of Federalism: The Disintegration of the Federalist Party, 1815-1830* (Princeton, 1962), pp. 134, 271.

7. Webster to Jeremiah Mason, February 14, 1825, *Writings and Speeches*, XVI, 100.

8. Charles Francis Adams (ed.), *The Memoirs of John Quincy Adams, Comprising Portions of His Diary from 1795 to 1848* (Philadelphia, 1874-1877), VII, 525. (Hereafter cited as Adams, *Memoirs*.)

9. Plumer, "Reminiscences of Daniel Webster," *Writings and Speeches*, XVII, 549.

10. Quoted in Paul Revere Frothingham, *Edward Everett, Orator and Statesman* (Boston, 1925), p. 121.

11. Elisha Whittlesey to Daniel Webster, September 14, 1833, Daniel Webster Papers, Manuscript Division, Library of Congress. (Hereafter cited as Webster Papers.)

12. The Carlyle quotation is in Thomas Carlyle to Ralph Waldo Emerson, June 24, 1839, Joseph Slater (ed.), *The Correspondence of Emerson and Carlyle* (New York, 1964), p. 240.

13. Charles Lanman, *The Private Life of Daniel Webster* (New York, 1852), p. 179.

14. Harriet Martineau, *A Retrospect of Western Travel* (London, 1838), I, 290, 300.

15. *Ibid.*, pp. 289-290.

16. Benjamin F. Perry, *Reminiscences of Public Men* (Philadelphia, 1883), pp. 64-65.

17. Oliver H. Smith, *Early Indiana Trials and Sketches. Reminiscences by Hon. O. H. Smith* (Cincinnati, 1858), p. 460.

18. Webster to Jeremiah Mason, February 27, 1830, *Writings and Speeches*, XVII, 488.

19. The speech is printed in *Writings and Speeches*, II, 3-75.

20. James Parton, *Life of Andrew Jackson* (New York, 1861), III, 282.

21. Webster to Jeremiah Mason, April 14, 1830, in Claude H. Van Tyne (ed.), *The Letters of Daniel Webster from Documents Owned Principally by the New Hampshire Historical Society* (New York, 1902), p. 152. (Hereafter cited as *Letters of Webster*.)

22. Madison to Daniel Webster, March 15, 1833, *Writings and Speeches*, I, 100-101.

23. [George Ticknor], "Review of Speeches and Forensic Arguments, by Daniel Webster," *American Quarterly Review*, IX (1831), 455. To meet the demand for a volume of Webster's speeches, his nephew, Professor Charles B. Haddock of Dartmouth College, published a one-volume collection entitled *Speeches and Forensic Arguments* (1831). In the same year, Samuel L. Knapp published *A Memoir of the Life of Daniel Webster* (Boston, 1831). Webster assisted Knapp in preparing the biography by supplying him with reminiscences (Fuess, *Daniel Webster*, I, 385).

24. [Thomas Hamilton], *Men and Manners in America*, 2nd ed. (Philadelphia, 1833), II, 78.

25. Lawrence to his son, March 6, 1830, in William R. Lawrence (ed.), *Extracts*

*from the Diary and Correspondence of the Late Amos Lawrence With a Brief Account of Some Incidents in His Life* (Boston, 1855), p. 97; Lawrence to Daniel Webster, October 23, 1830, *Writings and Speeches*, XVII, 507.

26. Fuess, *Daniel Webster*, I, 385. See also Henry Cabot Lodge, *Daniel Webster*, 3rd ed. (Boston, 1884), p. 207; Current, *Daniel Webster*, p. 72; Allan L. Benson, *Daniel Webster* (New York, 1929), p. 202; Frederic Austin Ogg, *Daniel Webster* (Philadelphia, 1914), p. 231.

27. George Ticknor Curtis, *Life of Daniel Webster*, 5th ed. (New York, 1893), I, 386-387.

28. Joseph Gales to Daniel Webster, March 27, 1831, *ibid.*, I, 398-399. See also Charles Miner to Daniel Webster, December 31, 1830, Webster Papers.

29. Webster to Henry Clay, May 29, 1830, *Writings and Speeches*, XVI, 198-199.

30. The abduction and suspected murder in 1826 of William Morgan, who had published a work revealing the secrets of Masonry, created intense excitement in the emotionally "Burned-over District" of western New York and culminated in the rise of an Antimasonic party pledged to the extirpation of all secret societies. The movement spread through the rural areas of the northern states, and under the direction of young and dynamic leaders such as Thurlow Weed and William H. Seward of New York, and Thaddeus Stevens of Pennsylvania, threatened to take over the constituency of the National Republican party. To his friend Jeremiah Mason, Webster wrote that "the Anti-Masonic party, steadily increasing in N. York, is breaking out like an Irish rebellion in Pennsylvania. It goes on with a force that subdues all other feeling. These things put party calculations at defiance" (March 19, 1830, *Writings and Speeches*, XVI, 194-195).

31. Curtis, *Life of Webster*, I, 393.

32. William W. Irwin to Daniel Webster, August 25, 1830, Webster Papers.

33. White to Daniel Webster, August 7, 1831, *Letters of Webster*, pp. 161-162.

34. Webster to Charles Miner, August 28, 1831, quoted in Charles Francis Richardson and Elizabeth Miner (Thomas) Richardson, *Charles Miner, A Pennsylvania Pioneer* (Wilkes-Barre, 1916), pp. 139-140.

35. Statement of Hiram Ketchum to George T. Curtis, quoted in Curtis, *Life of Webster*, I, 404; Fuess, *Daniel Webster*, II, 6; Ogg, *Webster*, pp. 235-236.

36. Curtis, *Life of Webster*, I, 398; Webster to Ambrose Spencer, November 16, 1831, *Writings and Speeches*, XVI, 214-216.

37. Webster to Nicholas Biddle, December 18, 1831, in Reginald C. McGrane (ed.), *The Correspondence of Nicholas Biddle Dealing With National Affairs, 1807-1844* (Boston, 1919), pp. 145-146. (Hereafter cited as *Biddle Correspondence.*)

38. For an excellent account of the Bank War as a "political phenomenon" see Robert V. Remini, *Andrew Jackson and the Bank War* (New York, 1967).

39. Edward Stanwood, *A History of the Presidency from 1788 to 1897*, new ed. (Boston, 1928), p. 164.

40. Quoted in Claude M. Fuess, *Rufus Choate: The Wizard of the Law* (New York, 1928), p. 80.

# THE WEBSTER-JACKSON RAPPROCHEMENT

**2** The growing support for the nullification doctrine in South Carolina put Webster on his guard, and he kept a wary eye on that state's actions. The publication of Calhoun's *South Carolina Exposition* (1828), he wrote Benjamin F. Perry in 1833, had convinced him that "the plan of a southern confederacy had been received with favor, by a great many of the political men of the South."[1] As South Carolina's attitude toward the protective tariff became more militant, Webster's concern increased. In October 1831, he told Henry Clay that he anticipated an attack on the Constitution at the next session of Congress: "Not only the Tariff, but the Constitution itself, in its elementary and fundamental provisions will be assailed with talent, vigor, and union. Everything is to be debated as if nothing had been settled."[2]

The passage of the Tariff of 1832, as Webster had feared, ushered in a period of national crisis. Although it reduced duties to the general level of 1824, the new tariff was totally unacceptable to the nullification party in South Carolina. On November 19, 1832, a state convention met at Columbia and adopted an ordinance nullifying the tariffs of 1828 and 1832. No tariff duties were to be collected within the state after February 1, 1833, and the convention warned that South Carolina would secede if the federal government made any effort to enforce the tariff law.[3]

Andrew Jackson's reply to South Carolina's defiance was a blending of conciliation and threat.[4] The President would support a lower tariff, but clearly would not yield to the Palmetto state's threats. In a "Proclamation to the People of South Carolina" (December 10, 1832), Jackson rejected nullification as "incompatible with the existence of the Union, contradicted expressly by the letter of the Constitution, unauthorized by its spirit, inconsistent with every principle on which it was founded, and destructive of the great object for which it was formed." A state could neither secede nor defy a federal law. "Disunion by armed force is *treason*," he thundered. "Are you ready to incur its guilt?"[5]

When Jackson issued his proclamation, Webster was in Boston preparing to return to Washington for the congressional session. The proclamation elicited his immediate approval; for it expounded a political theory so similar to his own as set forth in the debate with Hayne, that it was regarded at the time "as a manifest, but of course a very excusable, plagiarism."[6] Delaying his departure, he attended a public meeting at historic Faneuil Hall called to sustain the President's action, and delivered a short address. Webster warned that the secession of one state would mean the end of the Union and pledged his "entire and cordial support" for Jackson's announced policy of firmness. "The general principles of the proclamation are such as I entirely approve," he declared. "I esteem them to be the true principles of the Constitution."[7]

National Republicans generally applauded Jackson's position. The Cleveland *Western Reserve Chronicle* reported that the proclamation "was hailed as the harbinger of glad tidings by the opposers of the administration. . . . It is worthy of remark that the returning sanity of the President was hailed by spontaneous approbation."[8] Hartford Convention Federalists like Harrison

Gray Otis saw no inconsistency in endorsing the proclamation and were overjoyed at the discomfiture it gave to Jackson's state rights supporters. Otis chortled to a friend: "That it would be gall & wormwood to Virginia and to Jackson's friends generally, I *felt* the moment I had become satisfied of the genuineness of the proclamation & was equally persuaded that we of the old school should lose no time in expressing our approbation of our own principles, by whomsoever promulgated." "For my part I thank old Hicky," Otis confessed, "tho' I never conceived that such wholesome waters would come from a bitter fountain."[9]

Webster's decision to support the President had political implications that were not lost on either ally or foe. Friends of Webster believed Jackson's stand against nullification might ultimately lead to alliance with Webster from which the Massachusetts statesman might first gain a cabinet post and in time the presidency.[10] Thus the Boston *Gazette* thought Jackson's proclamation "a very fortunate document for Mr. Webster"; and predicted that if he played his cards skillfully, he could be "at the head of the administration party within twelve months."[11]

New England Democrats were alarmed by the eagerness with which Webster and his friends embraced the President's proclamation. Would they be sacrificed to secure National Republican support for Jackson's stand against nullification? The Concord *New Hampshire Patriot,* the organ of Senator Isaac Hill, a leader of the New England Democracy, told the President that he had a "thousand times more to fear" from the friendship of Webster and the Federalists than from "the open, armed hostility of all the nullifiers in the union." The price of such *"disinterested* patriotism," warned the *Patriot,* would be a new charter for the Bank of the United States, maintenance of a protective tariff, and the sacrifice of Martin Van Buren and Jackson's other early friends.[12] The Boston *Morning Post,* press spokesman of the Democratic machine in that city, noting the support of Otis and other former Federalists for Jackson's proclamation, declared that Hartford conventionists rebuking nullifiers was like "Satan rebuking sin."[13]

When Webster reached Washington, efforts were already

underway to solve the nullification crisis before South Carolina's deadline of February 1, 1833. On January 8 Gulian Verplanck of New York, chairman of the House Ways and Means Committee, reported a new tariff bill which made large immediate reductions in duties and proposed to lower them fifty per cent in 1834. The Verplanck bill was an administration measure in keeping with the promise implied in the proclamation to lower tariff duties. It was the only offer of accommodation to South Carolina which Jackson would countenance. Friends of Martin Van Buren, the Vice-President elect, urged speedy passage of the bill. The New Yorker had made his way to national eminence in alliance with the Old Republicans of the South, especially in Virginia; and the nullification crisis, by threatening to split the Democratic party along the Mason-Dixon line, was jeopardizing his hopes for the presidency.

Northern protectionists would not sacrifice their section's economic interests to save South Carolina from Jackson's wrath or pull Van Buren's political chestnuts from the fire; they stalled the Verplanck tariff in the House. Webster went into the House chamber on January 18, where several representatives told him they looked upon the bill as "already a corpse," although they might continue the debate for perhaps a week longer.[14] The President's friends supported the measure, but Webster believed Jackson personally did not wish the bill to pass. *"E contra,* I fancy he would prefer the undivided honor of suppressing nullification now, and to take his own time hereafter to remodel the tariff." Because the Jackson party in Congress feared the effect of the doctrines of the proclamation it was endeavoring to interpose and save South Carolina, "not by the proclamation, but by taking away the ground of complaint."[15]

While extending the "carrot" of the Verplanck tariff, Jackson was preparing to exercise the stick if South Carolina tried to enforce nullification. In December he wrote Joel R. Poinsett, a Unionist leader in South Carolina, that he was only waiting to be furnished with certified copies of the acts of the South Carolina legislature implementing the nullification ordinance before sending a message to Congress asking for the means to carry his proclamation into effect. "Within forty days, I can have within the limits of So. Carolina fifty thousand men, and in forty days more another fifty thousand," he assured Poinsett.[16] On January 16, 1833, he asked Congress for increased powers to execute the federal law in South Carolina. If Congress failed to act, Jackson was fully prepared to move without additional authority. ". . . Fear not," he assured Poinsett once more, *the union will be preserved, and treason and rebellion promptly put down, when and where it may shew its monster head.*"[17]

Webster was a member of the Senate Judiciary Committee which submitted the Revenue Collection Bill (the so-called "Force Bill") to the Senate on January 21, and he gave it his full support. He had already drafted a series of eight "Principles" which were to govern his conduct in the coming months, the first of which was "to sustain the administration in executing the laws; [and] to support all measures necessary . . . to counteract the proceedings of South Carolina," and the second "not to give up, or compromise, the *principle of protection.*"[18] He was well pleased with the President's message of January 16. It had produced "a strong sensation," he wrote Stephen White.

> People begin to see, at last, what Nullification is, and what must be done to put it down. It makes them look sober. Mr. Calhoun is highly excited. He acts as if he felt the whole world to be agt. him. . . . Looking upon Mr. C. and the whole party here, as completely prostrate, I confess I feel no disposition to treat them with unnecessary harshness, or censure. Mr. C. will certainly not provoke any thing personal, between himself and me, and, as certainly, I shall forbear from any personal unkindness towards him.[19]

Webster was frequently seen at the home of Secretary of State Edward Livingston during this period, and state rights leaders believed that he, and not the leading Jacksonians, would be the President's paladin in Congress. "The ultra federalists drive on these measures and Webster will be the great champion of the administration," Senator John Tyler of Virginia wrote to Governor John Floyd of that state on the day following the introduction of the Force Bill. "They must come into the closest

and most fraternal embrace. I dined at the Palace [White House],
yes, palace, a few days since, and found Mr. W. there in all his
glory."[20]

Matthew Davis, the "Spy in Washington," expressed a similar opinion in a letter from the capital:

> The echoes from the palace announce that Mr. Webster is con-
> sidered the staff on which reliance must be placed in the Senate.
> . . . At a moment, the most unexpected to him, to his friends,
> and to the country, he finds himself called upon to sustain the
> measures of the administration, on the ground that they are such
> as the federal party of 1798 would have sustained. . . . Yet a few
> days, and his influence with the President will be equaled by few,
> surpassed by none. . . . The Federalists, with a portion of the
> Clay men, have taken under their charge the measures of the
> administration. Mark what I say. Without these new allies Gen.
> Jackson would stand almost alone, in both Houses of Congress.[21]

But a reluctant champion entered the lists against the formidable Calhoun, who had resigned the vice-presidency to enter
the Senate. On January 22, the South Carolinian introduced a
series of resolutions justifying nullification; and Webster, hitherto
passive, was stirred to action. On January 28, he denied Calhoun's
allegations that the Force Bill established a military despotism
and announced that at the proper time he would try conclusions
with him on this point. Yet on February 3, he wrote Judge Joseph
Hopkinson that he had no wish to speak personally on Calhoun's
resolutions: "I should be more likely, I am sure, to lose than to
gain, by a new effort on these topics; yet, if we hear from Mr.
Calhoun, I shall attempt to answer him."[22]

On February 7, Senator William King of Alabama asked
Webster if he wished to express any sentiments on the Force Bill.
Webster replied he had "no disposition to address the Senate at
present, nor, under existing circumstances, at any other time, on
the subject of this bill." But on the following day, he spoke
briefly in its behalf and announced that as an independent member of the Senate, he would give a "hearty support to the administration, in all measures which I deem to be fair, just, and
necessary."[23]

When Jackson became dissatisfied with the progress of the Force Bill, he sent Edward Livingston to urge Webster to take the lead in opposing Calhoun. Webster agreed; and Livingston was able to assure the White House that when Calhoun addressed the Senate, Webster would answer him.[24] Yet despite this promise to the President, Webster was still reluctant to risk his reputation in a forensic duel with the brilliant Carolinian. "I wish not to speak, but it seems unavoidable," he wrote to Judge Hopkinson on the night before his speech. "Courage! I cannot better the matter of 1830—nor equal it—but I will try not to show evidence of senility."[25]

On February 15 and 16, Calhoun addressed the Senate in defense of his constitutional views and warned that if the Force Bill passed, it would be resisted to the death. When he had concluded his remarks shortly after one o'clock, Webster, who had ridden to the Capitol in the President's carriage, replied with another stout defense of national sovereignty. He contended that Calhoun's doctrine, if carried into effect, would make the present government no better than the old Confederation and would ruin the Republic. "I shall exert every faculty I possess," he declared in closing, "to prevent the Constitution from being nullified, destroyed, or impaired; and even should I see it fall, I will still, with a voice feeble, perhaps, but earnest as ever issued from human lips, and with fidelity and zeal which nothing shall extinguish, call on the *People* to come to the rescue." There was a spontaneous burst of applause from the gallery.[26] Major William Lewis, one of Jackson's intimates, attended the debate and hurried word of Webster's speech to the President. Jackson was highly pleased. "Mr. Webster replied to Mr. Calhoun yesterday," he wrote Poinsett, "and it is said demolished him. . . . Mr. Webster handled him as a child."[27] Webster's friends also claimed another triumph for the "Godlike Daniel."

Webster's speech in reply to Calhoun was his only major oratorical effort during the debate on the Force Bill, as he left to others the day to day defense of the measure on the floor of the Senate. Nevertheless, he did what he could to secure its speedy passage. When State Rights Democrats attempted to stall the bill's progress by frequent motions to adjourn for the day, Webster strongly objected. On February 7, he told the Senate that if the Force Bill were to be acted upon it could only be done by sitting late, and he announced that he would vote against any motion to adjourn before five or six o'clock until final action had been taken. Later, he was violently assailed by Senator George Poindexter of Mississippi, one of the nullification party in the Senate, who contrasted Webster's opposition to the War of 1812 with his support of Jackson in 1833, and suggested that he had earlier been guilty of treachery, cowardice, or both. Webster was grievously offended, but did not deign to reply, whereupon Poindexter declared that he "felt the most perfect contempt for the Senator from Massachusetts." At the end of the session, Clay, in his familiar role of pacificator, arranged a reconciliation between the two men.[28]

On February 20, when the long debate on the Force Bill finally ended, Webster had the honor of calling for the yeas and nays on final passage. Thirty-two senators voted in favor while John Tyler was the only senator present voting no. Both Clay and Calhoun found it convenient to be absent when the vote was taken. Twenty-three of twenty-four northern senators voted yes, an indication of strong popular approval in that section for the President's firm stand against nullification. Only nine of twenty-four southern senators were recorded as favoring the measure.[29]

Webster's support of the Force Bill in the Senate produced a *rapprochement* with the President as the bitterness aroused in the Bank War subsided. Jackson had a reputation as a man who cherished his hatreds, but he could extend the hand of friendship when policy demanded (as witness his reconciliation with Thomas Hart Benton); and he was ready to forgive Webster for his support of Biddle and the Bank in 1832. The President was shrewd enough to realize that he might use the ambitious New Englander to counter Clay and Calhoun and keep the opposition off balance. He quickly thanked Webster for his aid, and Livingston added his own warm thanks. Before the end of the session, an eastern senator of Jackson's party asked Webster to look over a list of applicants for office in the East and to strike off those displeasing to him! Webster, of course, declined.[30]

The possibility that Webster might accept a cabinet post was canvassed in the nation's press; and it was hinted that upon the anticipated retirement of John Marshall, he would be appointed Chief Justice of the Supreme Court.[31] When a Democratic source objected that the party could not forget Webster's Federalist antecedents, the Cincinnati *Daily Gazette* replied that this was a minor difficulty. "Mr. Webster can be as easily 'dyed in wool' as Mr. Louis McLane, if he will only consent to the necessary immersion."[32]

While Webster drew closer to Jackson in their common fight against nullification, he and Henry Clay were growing apart because of the latter's stand on the tariff. Clay did not share Webster's enthusiasm for Jackson's proclamation. "There are some things in it," he wrote to Francis Brooke, "entirely too ultra for me, and which I cannot stomach."[33] Dislike and distrust of Jackson, jealousy of Webster, a desire to recoup the prestige lost in his recent defeat, the possibility of a political alliance with Calhoun, all played a part in turning Clay's thoughts to the possibility of a compromise on the tariff which would satisfy South Carolina.[34]

When the Verplanck bill was introduced, Clay was apprehensive of its passage and began to consult on a new measure with manufacturers and members of Congress, including John Tyler and John C. Calhoun. The introduction of the Force Bill, which Clay reluctantly supported, spurred on the negotiations. An agreement was worked out between Clay and Calhoun in which the Kentuckian agreed to a gradual reduction in all duties to the revenue level and to the abandonment of the principle of protection; Calhoun, on his part, pledged to support Clay's tariff bill and secure repeal of the nullification ordinance.[35]

On February 12, Clay presented his compromise proposal. It provided for a gradual reduction of duties until they should stand at a uniform twenty per cent on July 1, 1842. Clay argued it would give adequate protection for nine years, restore harmony and avert the dangers of civil war, and separate the tariff from politics. When he had finished, Calhoun announced he would support the bill.[36]

Friends of Webster and Jackson saw in this understanding on the tariff the inauguration of a new political alliance between the head of nullification and the head of the American system.[37] Protectionists were astonished by what the Philadelphia *National Gazette* called Clay's "great leap across the Potowmac [sic]."[38] "The great champion of the American System has united with Mr. Calhoun," Associate Justice Joseph Story wrote Judge Hopkinson. "The protective system and the constitutional power to protect are to be abandoned. Instead of a sudden destruction of life at a single blow [the Verplanck tariff], the patient is to be slowly bled to death. We have all been in amazement. . . ."[39]

In the Senate, Webster rallied colleagues from protectionist centers, including George M. Dallas of Pennsylvania and Asher Robbins of Rhode Island, against Clay's tariff bill. He viewed the measure as a sacrifice of New England's manufacturing interests and a base yielding to the threats of a single state. Where South Carolina was concerned he preferred the sword to the olive branch. When Clay first broached the idea of a compromise on the tariff, Webster declared that "it would be yielding great principles to faction; and that the time had come to test the strength of the constitution and the government."[40] On February 25, he denounced the tariff bill because it attempted to bind future Congresses, in respect to the measure of protection to be given manufacturers; because it called for uniform rather than specific duties; and because it surrendered the constitutional power of protection.

All his massive oratory availed nothing. Clay's compromise bill passed the Senate on March 1, 1833, by a vote of twenty-nine to sixteen, Webster voting no, and the House concurred. The Force Bill passed the House at the same time and Jackson signed both measures on March 2. South Carolina defiantly nullified the Force Bill but wisely accepted the compromise tariff, and for the moment at least, civil war was averted. On reflection, Webster was fairly well satisfied with the result. He wrote William Sullivan on April 19: "All things have not happened as I could wish;

but on the whole, I think the events of the winter have tended to strengthen the union of the States, and to uphold the government. But it has many and powerful enemies, not easily subdued, and never to be reconciled."[41]

Webster was greatly angered by Clay's seeming apostasy on the tariff and a noticeable coolness developed between the two men. Clay complained to Nicholas Biddle after Congress adjourned: "As for *your* friend M. W. [Mr. Webster] (he is determined not to allow me to consider him *mine*) nothing that I can do seems right in his eyes; whilst others can do nothing wrong."[42] Webster was so embittered by the passage of Clay's tariff that even ten years later he recalled there was "no measure ever passed by Congress during my connection with that body that caused me so much grief and mortification. . . . The principle was bad, the measure was bad, the consequences were bad."[43] When Congress adjourned, he took the notes of his speeches against the tariff bill to Philadelphia, where he began to write them out for publication. A friend, possibly Biddle, dissuaded him from the action, claiming that the deed was done; the speeches would only widen differences between friends. Webster acquiesced but later regretted not publishing them.[44]

Clearly the Massachusetts senator was restive and unhappy in his political alliance with Clay, and with good reason. If the Clay-Calhoun coalition should endure, his own hopes for a presidential nomination in 1836 would be seriously jeopardized. Calhoun and his friends would never support a New England nationalist for the presidency, but they might support the accommodating Henry Clay. As Webster saw it, New England's interests had already been sacrificed to save Calhoun and his state from Jackson's wrath; and the South Carolinian would exact further concessions for any future service to Clay. And the very thought of a political alliance with the arch-nullifier repelled one whose reputation rested upon hymns to national supremacy and the glorious Union.

On the other hand, Webster shared Jackson's views on nullification, and his firm support of the proclamation and the Force Bill had won him the President's thanks. A union with Jackson in a new party openly dedicated to nationalist principles might offer more congenial bonds and greater opportunity for personal advancement than grudging support of Clay and his new ally, Calhoun. Rumors of a realignment of parties had been circulating almost from the day that Webster had endorsed Jackson's proclamation, and the coming months were to demonstrate clearly that such a realignment was a possibility.

## NOTES

*1.* Webster to Benjamin F. Perry, April 10, 1833, *Writings and Speeches*, XVII, 535.

*2.* Webster to Henry Clay, October 5, 1831, in Calvin Colton (ed.), *The Private Correspondence of Henry Clay* (New York, 1855), p. 318. (Hereafter cited as *Clay Correspondence*.)

*3.* For the nullification crusade see William W. Freehling, *Prelude to Civil War: The Nullification Controversy in South Carolina, 1816-1836* (New York, 1966).

*4.* Glyndon Van Deusen, *The Jacksonian Era, 1828-1848* (New York, 1959), p. 73.

*5.* James D. Richardson, *A Compilation of the Messages and Papers of the Presidents, 1789-1897* (Washington, 1896-1899), II, 640-656.

*6.* Ben: Perley Poore, *Perley's Reminiscences of Sixty Years in the National Metropolis* (Philadelphia, 1886), I, 139.

*7.* Curtis, *Life of Webster,* I, 590-592; Washington *National Intelligencer*, December 22, 1832, quoting Boston *Daily Advertiser and Patriot*, December 18, 1832.

*8.* Eber Malcolm Carroll, *Origins of the Whig Party* (Durham, 1925), p. 74, quoting Cleveland *Western Reserve Chronicle*, n.d.

*9.* Otis to George Harrison, February 20, 1833, quoted in Samuel Eliot Morison, *The Life and Letters of Harrison Gray Otis, Federalist, 1765-1848* (Boston, 1913), II, 292-293.

*10.* Current, *Daniel Webster*, p. 78.

*11.* J. C. Fitzpatrick (ed.), "Autobiography of Martin Van Buren," *Annual Report of the American Historical Association*, II (1918), 680, quoting Boston *Gazette*, n.d. (Hereafter cited as Fitzpatrick, "Autobiography.")

*12.* Niles' *Weekly Register*, XLIII (1833), 346, quoting *New Hampshire Patriot*, n.d.

*13.* Arthur B. Darling, *Political Changes in Massachusetts, 1824-1848* (New Haven, 1925), p. 149, quoting Boston *Morning Post*, n.d.

*14.* Webster to Stephen White, January 18, 1833, "Letter of Daniel Webster, 1833," *American Historical Review*, XXV (1920), 696. (Hereafter cited as "Letter of Webster.")

*15.* Webster to William Sullivan, January 3, 1833, quoted in Curtis, *Life of Webster*, I, 437.

*16.* Jackson to Joel R. Poinsett, December 9, 1832, in John Spencer Bassett (ed.), *The Correspondence of Andrew Jackson* (Washington, 1926-1933), IV, 498. (Hereafter cited as *Jackson Correspondence.*)

*17.* Jackson to Joel R. Poinsett, January 24, 1833, *ibid.*, V, 11.

*18.* "Principles," *Writings and Speeches*, XV, 104-105. George F. Hoar, to whom this manuscript once belonged, wrote the following upon it: "This paper was probably drawn up by Mr. Webster about the beginning of the session of December 1832. Some of its language is found in his speech of February 8, 1833" (p. 104).

*19.* Webster to Stephen White, January 18, 1833, "Letter of Webster," p. 696.

*20.* Louise Livingston Hunt, *Memoir of Mrs. Edward Livingston: With Letters Hitherto Unpublished* (New York, 1886), p. 103; Tyler to John Floyd, January 22, 1833, "Original Letters," *William and Mary College Quarterly Historical Magazine*, XXI (1912), 11.

*21.* Carroll, *Whig Party*, p. 77n, quoting *Morning Courier and New York Enquirer*, February 2, 1833.

*22.* Webster to Joseph Hopkinson, February 2, [1833], quoted in William M. Meigs, *The Life of John Caldwell Calhoun* (New York, 1917), II, 12.

*23.* *Register of Debates in Congress*, 22nd Cong., 2nd Sess. (Washington, 1833), IX, part 1, 404, 410-411. (Hereafter cited as *Register of Debates* with appropriate numeration); Curtis, *Life of Webster*, I, 440.

*24.* Charles March, *Daniel Webster and His Contemporaries*, 4th ed. (New York, 1859), pp. 198-200; William Hatcher, *Edward Livingston: Jeffersonian Republican and Jacksonian Democrat* (Baton Rouge, 1940), p. 390.

*25.* Webster to Joseph Hopkinson [February 15, 1833], quoted in Meigs, *Life of Calhoun*, II, 13.

*26. Writings and Speeches*, VI, 181-231; *Register of Debates* 22nd Cong., 2nd Sess., IX, part 1, 587.

*27.* Claude G. Bowers, *The Party Battles of the Jackson Period* (Boston, 1922), p. 275; Jackson to Joel R. Poinsett, February 17, 1833, *Jackson Correspondence*, V, 18.

*28. Register of Debates*, 22nd Cong., 2nd Sess., IX, part 1, 404-405, 602-661, 810-812.

*29. Ibid.*, p. 688.

*30.* Curtis, *Life of Webster*, I, 464.

*31.* James Louis Petigru to Hugh S. Legare, March 5, 1833, quoted in James Petigru Carson, *Life, Letters and Speeches of James Louis Petigru: The Union Man of South Carolina* (Washington, 1920), p. 121.

*32.* Carroll, *Whig Party*, p. 81, quoting Cincinnati *Daily Gazette*, February 21, 1833.

*33.* Clay to Francis Brooke, December 12, 1832, *Clay Correspondence*, p. 345.

*34.* Glyndon G. Van Deusen, *The Life of Henry Clay* (Boston, 1939), pp. 265-266.

*35.* Charles Maurice Wiltse, *John C. Calhoun* (Indianapolis, 1944-1951), II, 184-186.

*36.* Van Deusen, *Henry Clay,* p. 268; Wiltse, *Calhoun,* II, 185.

*37.* Albany *Argus,* February 26, 1833.

*38.* Philadelphia *National Gazette,* March 1, 1833.

*39.* Joseph Story to Joseph Hopkinson, February 17, 1833, quoted in Meigs, *Life of Calhoun,* II, 26.

*40.* Curtis, *Life of Webster,* I, 453; Thomas Hart Benton, *Thirty Years' View: or, A History of the Working of the American Government for Thirty Years from 1820 to 1850* (New York, 1856), I, 342.

*41.* Webster to William Sullivan, April 19, 1833, *Writings and Speeches,* XVII, 537.

*42.* Clay to Nicholas Biddle, March 4, 1833, Nicholas Biddle Papers, Manuscript Division, Library of Congress. (Hereafter cited as Biddle Papers.)

*43. Writings and Speeches,* III, 131.

*44.* Webster to Hiram Ketchum, January 20, 1836, quoted in Curtis, *Life of Webster,* I, 455-456.

# THE
# CONSTITUTION
# AND THE UNION

**3** During the winter of 1832-1833, the possibility of a realignment of parties upon the issue of maintaining federal authority was a constant topic of discussion among political leaders and in the press. As early as November 2, 1832, Amos Kendall, a close adviser to the President, had written Van Buren that the Bank would be considered dead as soon as Jackson's triumphant re-election was ascertained, and that "all men of all parties in the northern, middle and western states may be united upon the question of the *Union against Nullification,* and an immense majority of the South may be rallied in the same cause. On this basis the National Republicans in the northern and middle states may be willing to unite with the friends of the administration."[1] Webster's cooperation with Jackson in passing the Force Bill and his sharp disagreement with Clay over the tariff added impetus to this intriguing possibility. "Recent political events make it plain that parties must be taken into a new draft," declared the Salem (Mass.) *Gazette.* "The late combinations have been completely broken up. . . . *Clay* and

*Calhoun* have combined Nullification and National Republican-
ism—the *West* and the *South* are henceforth in close alliance, and
the National Republicans of the Free States are henceforth ex-
cluded. . . ."²

P. P. F. Degrand wrote to Nicholas Biddle from Boston that
ever since the appearance of Jackson's proclamation, he had believed that the President's stand against state rights *"would
necessarily ultimately lead to an alliance, offensive and defensive,
between Jackson* and the Party that goes against the mis-called
State Rights;—for the judiciary;—for internal improvements;—for
the tariff; and for the bank. . . ."³

After Clay reached agreement with Calhoun on the compromise tariff, a disgruntled Webster schemed to supplant the Kentuckian as head of the National Republican party and to carry
its members into a coalition with Jackson on a "Constitution and
Union" platform. In such a party, Webster would naturally ex-
pect the position of heir apparent.⁴ Eli Davis, a journalist, wrote
to Webster from Leesburg, Virginia, on March 27, 1833, that
"wherever I go the people appear pleased at the idea that you
are to be substituted as a candidate for the Presidency in lieu of
Mr. Clay. . . . They say he deceived them by betraying their
interests to subserve Calhoun and now they would prefer you."
Plans were being formulated to establish a newspaper favorable to
Webster's candidacy: "It has been strongly urged by gentlemen of
high respectability and influence that our press ought to be lo-
cated at Washington and that after fixing upon a person to be run
as Vice President on the ticket with you as President, a position
shd. be immediately taken from which the whole ground of the
Union party and the friends of the tariff could be [reviewed?] in
a manner so as gradually to unite them in the support of this
ticket." Davis was negotiating with a Mr. Anderson in Washington for a press "complete in every respect" and if he decided to
establish the paper in that city, he would go himself to Boston
or send an agent to obtain subscriptions. "This letter is written
in confidence," he warned, "& is intended only for the eyes of your
confidential friends."⁵

In a letter forwarded to Webster, Dr. Edward Bryson of

Maryland expressed pleasure that Webster's friends intended to "bring him out." "The stand which he took last winter in relation to the subject of nulification [sic] together with his talents as a statesman," he added, "render it more than probable that should he be brought out that he will get almost the unanimous vote of our state—By all means let his annunciation be done speedily, we want a rallying point now is the propitious time."[6]

Clay was already aware of this movement among Webster's "confidential friends" to supplant him with the Massachusetts senator. He told Nicholas Biddle that after the introduction of the compromise tariff, "it was manifest at Washington that a few of the eastern friends of Mr. W., supposing that I had taken a step that would destroy me in the public estimation, indulged hopes that a new party would be formed, of which he might be sole head."[7] According to Martin Van Buren, Clay's friend despite their political differences, the Kentuckian suspected that Webster had left Washington in the spring of 1833 with two settled purposes in mind:

> first, to supplant him in the affection and confidence of their own party and, secondly, to conciliate the good will of President Jackson and as many of his friends as . . . practicable, with the ulterior design of employing one or the other or both of these means, incongruous as they might appear to be, to secure his own elevation to the Presidential office at the approaching and certain vacancy. . . .[8]

Clay, of course, would oppose such a design so threatening to his own political prospects with all the consummate political craft at his command, and he took the precaution of having his friend, Senator Peleg Sprague of Maine, tarry in New York City, Providence, and Boston, on his way home from Washington, to explain the merits of the new tariff to the leading National Republican politicians and businessmen. He was otherwise content to declare that the rift between himself and Webster had been closed.[9]

Powerful elements in the Democratic party also opposed any permanent understanding between Jackson and the senator from Massachusetts. The *New Hampshire Patriot,* press spokesman for Senator Isaac Hill, vehemently denied that the administration wanted Webster's support. Webster, said the paper scornfully, was "playing the sycophant—fawning about the President and tendering support to his administration at a time when his support is not wanted." He was like "the *spaniel* who licks the hand that beats him."[10] Yet the very violence of the *Patriot's* denial revealed concern that the personal ties between Jackson and Webster might lead to closer political ties with a resulting loss of government patronage for the Democratic faithful in New England.

Equally outspoken in opposition was the Albany *Argus,* organ of Van Buren's Albany Regency. It vigorously denied an assertion by the New York *Courier and Enquirer* that the Vice-President and Webster would form a "grand league" looking toward 1836.[11] Many persons incorrectly assumed that Van Buren, as the "heir to the throne," would welcome an arrangement between Jackson or himself and Webster for the latter's support in the coming campaign. Actually the wily "Little Magician" viewed such an association as a menace to his own election and maneuvered to keep Jackson and Webster apart.[12] When Amos Kendall in 1832 suggested a union of the administration and the National Republicans of the northern and middle states against nullification, Van Buren had replied that to court or meet their advances would strengthen the nullifiers in the South. Kendall had then agreed that "Webster and Calhoun and their immediate relatives, must be held at arms length on either side," although he still believed that among the rank and file of the Nationals there were many "honest men and good republicans" who might be won over.[13]

A Webster-Jackson alliance could only be consummated if the nullification issue remained sufficiently threatening to override these personal considerations; and in the spring and summer of 1833, there seemed a fair chance that this would prove the case. Portions of the Jackson press as well as papers friendly to Webster sounded the tocsin against the nullifiers, declared that the danger from their schemes was not over, and urged the people to rally to the embattled Union. The Philadelphia *National*

*Gazette,* pro-Webster and which had opposed the compromise tariff, told its readers that the nullifiers were "constant and strenuous in their efforts to extend their influence and make proselytes in the South and Southwestern States, in order to prepare them for a separate Confederacy." The Washington *Globe,* press voice of the administration, charged that the nullifiers hoped to combine the elements of discord in the South, "so as to produce a collision and appeal to arms, which may result in a league of States south of the Potomac—a secession from the Union—and finally a new confederacy."[14]

Unionist leaders privately voiced similar warnings. Jackson wrote his old comrade-in-arms, John Coffee, that the coalition of Clay, Calhoun, George Poindexter, and the nullifiers in the South must be met, "for be assured these men would do any act to destroy the union, and form a southern confederacy bounded, north, by the Patomac [sic] river. . . ."[15] In the spring of 1833, Webster believed that the danger was not over, and that the nullifiers would mount a bold attack against the "just and constitutional powers of the Government." "If I do not mistake," he wrote Joel R. Poinsett, "the question of paramount importance in our affairs is likely to be, for some time to come, *the preservation of the Union, or its dissolution;* and no power can decide this question but that of the people themselves. Let the question be argued—let it be discussed—give the people light, and they will decide right." The friends of the Union everywhere had an "indispensable duty" to exert themselves for its preservation and to act in harmony and with concert.[16]

Convinced that the President's decided stand against nullification had "scotched the snake, but not killed it," Unionists thought of organizing a national Union party to curb the nullifiers. Poinsett told Jackson that he was disposed "to form a party in all the states . . . which may be called in to the aid of the friends of the Union in any state where the Monster Disunion may show his head, whether in the form of nullification or in any other hideous shape."[17] In a letter to Webster, Poinsett warned that Calhoun and his friends were plotting the dissolution of the Union and unless the Union men exerted themselves for its preservation and acted with united councils against them, they would ultimately succeed.[18] The Philadelphia *National Gazette* echoed this suggestion that the Unionists should organize. It urged that "Union societies" be organized in every state to frustrate the "machinations" of the nullifiers. The paper suggested that "common national principles—a common constitutional creed—might be formally adopted, to which all true federal and national republicans could rally."[19]

The first fruits of the call for a close cooperation between northern and southern Unionists came in May 1833, after Congress had adjourned. Union men believed the nullifiers were deliberately agitating the explosive slavery question to foster discord between North and South. The constant harping of Duff Green's *United States Telegraph,* together with other state rights papers, on the growing number of anti-slavery societies in the North gave the Unionists some grounds for their fears. The Washington *Globe* declared that from "plain indications, it is now certain, that those who wish to produce a dissolution of the Union, will seek that result through the agitation of the Slave Question."[20] Poinsett warned Webster that the nullifiers were striving to excite the fear and jealousy of the South on the slavery question and could only be counteracted by prudent forbearance on the part of the non-slaveholding states.[21]

Even before receiving Poinsett's letter, Webster had decided to reassure the southern people that the North had no hostile intentions toward them on the slavery question. On May 16, 1833, he met with John Bolton, a Georgia Unionist, in New York City, and the two men agreed to a formal exchange of letters on the slavery question, the letters to be made public immediately. Bolton forthwith addressed a letter to Webster asking him to state his views as to the power of Congress over slavery, "and also as to the existence of any wish or design on the part of northern men, to interfere in any way with the security or regulation of that species of property." Webster's views, he concluded, would be communicated to "a distinguished friend of mine" in Georgia and through him to the public at large.[22]

Webster immediately replied that while his views on the

subject had already been declared he did not object to repeating them to help "friends of the Union and the Constitution, in the South," dispel prejudices and prevent unnecessary agitation. Webster said domestic slavery was a subject within the exclusive control of the states; Congress had no authority to interfere either in the emancipation or treatment of slaves. While slavery was considered a great moral and political evil in the North, any remedy must come from the southern states themselves. Imputations made against the North on these grounds lacked just foundation.[23]

In publishing this correspondence, the Savannah *Georgian* rebuked Calhoun and his nullifying friends for their efforts to agitate the slavery question for their own political aggrandizement. Webster, said the paper, was head of the "federal party" in the North, and his opinions reflected those of the party at large. The Washington *Globe* hailed Webster's letter as " 'a *wet blanket'* to the hopes of the incendiaries."[24] The exchange of letters thus served a two-fold purpose. It reassured southern Union men that northern brethren had no intention of interfering with domestic slavery and thus prevented any split between them on this question. It also indicated to southerners that Webster, if elected President, would respect their property in slaves.

A more serious obstacle to a new party alignment was Jackson's irrational prejudice against the Bank. Could Webster surmount this difficulty? Foes of a Webster-Jackson union thought not. "Nothing lacks now to complete the love-feast, but for Jackson and Webster to solemnize the coalition with a few mint julips," Isaac Hill sneeringly wrote Thomas Hart Benton, "But never fear, my friend. This mixing of oil and water is only the temporary shakeup of Nullification. Wait till Jackson gets at the Bank again, and then the scalping knives will glisten once more."[25]

To further complicate matters, the Washington *Globe* was associating the Bank with the nullification conspiracy: "The Bank supports the nullifiers and the nullifiers the Bank." The success of these allies would prove fatal. Whether the government was overthrown by force, or undermined by corruption, the ruin,

however effected, would be irreparable. The *Globe* charged that
the Bank was supplying the nullifiers with a secret service fund to
start or buy up newspapers in the South.[26] Jackson shared and
perhaps inspired these views. Speaking of the Clay-Calhoun
coalition with its allies among the few Virginia nullifiers and the
Poindexter men in the South and Southwest, the President fumed
that "this combination wields the U. States Bank, and with its
corrupting influence they calculate to carry every thing, even its
recharter by two thirds of congress, against the veto of the executive." If they succeeded, "with this hydra of corruption, they
will rule the nation, and its charter will be perpetual and its
corrupting influence destroy the liberty of our country."[27]

Jackson's hostility to the Bank would have to be overcome if
Webster was to prolong his cooperation with the ultimate aim of
forming a new party on the Union issue. While such a timely
conversion was unlikely, given the tenacity with which Old Hickory adhered to his prejudices, there was some reason to believe it
was not impossible. A number of Jackson's associates in the
Democratic party were sympathetic to the Bank, including three
cabinet officers—Edward Livingston, Louis McLane, and Lewis
Cass, while Webster himself remained on good terms with the
President. Moreover, Nicholas Biddle was prepared to encourage
this new intimacy since he believed that when Webster had rallied
to Jackson's support he had established a claim to his gratitude
which might be used to gain a new charter for the Bank.[28] At the
same time, Biddle exerted his influence to prevent an open rup-
ture between Webster and Clay, in order to preserve the National
Republican party as a political force in the event Webster's overtures should fail.

When the Massachusetts senator arrived in Philadelphia on
March 19, after Congress had adjourned, many of his friends
wanted to give him a public dinner; but this Biddle discouraged,
because, as he explained to Clay, "I feared that it might oblige
him to say more on that subject [the compromise tariff] than it
is prudent to express at the present time, and because it would
probably furnish an occasion for his less discreet friends to do and
to say things excusable at a moment of excitement, but which

might afterward be regretted." Instead, Biddle substituted a large meeting of gentlemen at his own house, where Webster's friends could see him without forcing him to make a statement on any subject. Biddle candidly told Webster why he had prevented a public dinner, "in the propriety of which he entirely acquiesced." "In short," Biddle concluded, "he has left us two days ago, in a frame of mind entirely satisfactory, and your mutual friends seem to understand each other perfectly, that there ought not to be, and that there shall not be, any alienation between you, however you may have differed on one measure of policy."[29]

Conciliation could not be delayed for long. Secretary of the Treasury McLane was to succeed Livingston in the State Department, with the latter going to France as American minister; and there was much speculation as to McLane's successor and Jackson's next move against the Bank. The President was known to be considering removing government deposits as a final blow to the "Monster," and by early April, Webster feared that Jackson had settled upon removal "as a thing to be done" and "may be looking out for somebody willing to do the deed."[30] Biddle was more sanguine, but while he did not think Jackson would *"dare"* to remove the deposits, he saw no reason to take unnecessary chances. ". . . it is very desirable that whatever is done in the way of pacification should be done soon," he warned Webster, who was then in New York City, "for if the deposits are withdrawn, it will be a declaration of war which cannot be recalled. . . ." He advised Webster to make overtures to the administration through Edward Livingston who was expected in New York City within a few days.[31]

Webster had already written Livingston on March 21 to suggest a conference for a "confidential (interchange) upon topics which must arise, in the course of a short time, & on which public men will be obliged to act"—an oblique reference to the Bank question. He suggested the two men meet in New York City sometime in April.[32] Webster was in the city in early April with the intention of meeting the Secretary. Livingston, however, did not come and Webster wrote to Biddle from Boston that "I hear nothing yet, from Mr. L." A week later he wrote again from

Boston that he had still heard nothing from him. He thought the Secretary was occupied with an inquiry in regard to the burning of the treasury building.[33]

While Webster was denied an opportunity to talk with Livingston in New York, he arranged with Campbell P. White, a Democratic member of the House from that city, to have his views upon the question of the deposits reported to Jackson.[34] When White returned from Washington, he told Webster that the removal question was still far from settled. "I think it clear that Mr. McLane & Mr. Van Buren are decidedly *agt* the removal, & that the President is still pressing it," Webster informed Biddle. "A month's longer delay, I should think, would settle the question for this summer, if no new occurrence should arise."[35]

After his return to Boston, Webster warned the administration through "one of the most considerable Jackson men" in Massachusetts that the removal of the deposits would "create warm opposition at the North, & drive those, who would willingly support Genl. J. in all just measures, back to the arms of C. [Clay] and C. [Calhoun]."[36] He thus brought to Jackson's attention, through Democratic channels, the price that would have to be paid for his continued support of the administration. At the same time, however, his motives were not restricted to the sole desire to serve the Bank, for personal interest had an equal if not greater weight in his desire to reach an understanding on the Bank question. Louis McLane thought a Jackson-Webster merger "altogether probable" even if no agreement on the Bank was forthcoming. He wrote James Buchanan that "on the part of Webster's friends, it is ardently desired and incessantly urged; on his own part he affects to consider the President's hostility to the bank as the only barrier." But McLane was well aware of Webster's presidential ambitions and added cynically that he considered this "only the last qualm of a frail lady, who notwithstanding finally falls into the arms of the seducer."[37]

Another member of Jackson's immediate entourage, Major William B. Lewis, his close friend and former campaign manager, also thought that Webster would not look with disfavor on a coalition with the President. Moreover, Lewis himself was not adverse to such an arrangement. Although he would not "court" Webster, he wrote to James A. Hamilton, "I think we should not treat him or his friends harshly. I would not *invite,* nor would I repel any man or set of men. If they think proper to adopt our principles and fall in with us, I say let them do so." Lewis also thought Clay would not be the candidate of the National Republican party at the next election, and doubted that Webster was disposed "longer to sail under that flag." "So far it has proven to be an ensign of defeat and mortification to him and his friends," he noted. "I feel confident, if circumstances permit, he will haul it down and run up another. Whether the new one will be a Webster, or Van Buren, or McLane flag, I know not."[38]

Jackson's visit to New England in the summer of 1833 at the same time that Webster was touring the West showed that a new party alignment was possible. At the height of the nullification crisis, the Massachusetts legislature, on the motion of Webster's friend, Stephen White, had invited Jackson to visit the state; and Lewis Cass wrote to Webster on April 17, that the President would be in New England about June 20.[39] Webster replied that while he planned to tour the West, he would make every effort to be back in Boston by June 20 to greet Jackson "and to extend to him and his party the hospitalities of my house, as well as to unite with my friends and neighbors in such manifestations of respect as are due to him. . . ."[40] However, Webster was still on his travels when Jackson reached Boston.

Webster began his western tour from New York City in mid-May 1833. With his wife, daughter, and Stephen White, he went by steamboat up the Hudson River to Albany, the state capital. A large number of citizens waited upon him at his lodgings to pay their respects to the "distinguished champion of the Supremacy of the Constitution." At Albany, White and the ladies returned to Boston while Webster continued west through the lush Genesee Valley to Buffalo.[41] At this thriving port on Lake Erie, a committee tendered a public dinner, which he declined because of a desire to devote his time to Buffalo's interesting objects, "and to an unrestrained and unceremonious intercourse with its citizens." He did accept an invitation to witness the launching of a new steamboat, the *Daniel Webster,* at Black Rock.[42]

The *New Hampshire Patriot* charged that Webster was making an electioneering tour of the West to prepare the way for the next presidential canvass. "He wishes to be a candidate for President," declared the *Patriot,* "and to be supported as the great champion of the constitution, against the heresies of South Carolina Nullification. . . ."[43] This accusation was not too wide of the mark. Political motives inspired his trip. While in Buffalo, Webster talked with Albert Tracy, Jr., a leader in New York's Antimasonic party, and Tracy's report on this conversation to Thurlow Weed threw a bright light on Webster's political hopes at this time:

> [Webster] is infatuated with the notion . . . that the great approaching political division of the whole country is to be between Unionists and anti-Unionists. . . . Now, a plan which he suggests is that there be established at Utica a paper devoted to this question almost exclusively, and which he said could be made very strong and interesting by regular contributions from the Massachusetts delegation in Congress. . . . My standing objection to the whole of it is that it inevitably looks to Webster being a candidate for the next presidency, which . . . I regard as utterly unwise and hopeless.[44]

Webster and his friends clearly hoped to establish a group of such papers in the northern states to promote his candidacy on a Constitution and Union platform. His western tour was in part an effort to build popular support for this new political realignment. At the same time, he could not openly advocate a Union party, for this would have instantly severed his connection with Henry Clay before he reached any definite agreement with Jackson. Thus, while presumably canvassing the possibility of a new party in private conferences with western leaders, Webster limited his public remarks to generous praise of the President's stand against nullification and a vigorous defense of the protective tariff. To attract the West, he frequently avowed devotion to federal aid for internal improvements. Conspicuously absent was mention of the Bank of the United States.[45]

Since the destruction of existing party lines was essential to forming a new Union party, Webster carefully stressed the nonpartisan nature of his tour. He went West, not as a political partisan, not as a National Republican, but as a symbol of the Constitution and the Union. In his public meetings, everything of a political tendency was avoided as much as possible; the phrase, "without distinction of party," occurs with monotonous regularity in newspaper accounts. As the Washington *National Intelligencer* explained to its readers, Webster's welcome was on "purely national and patriotic" grounds: "It is for *his devotion to the stability of the Union,* that Mr. Webster is honored by the whole-souled people of the West."[46] Still some observers noted that the Jackson party was "peculiarly zealous to do him honor."[47]

When Webster reached Cincinnati in mid-June, after visiting briefly in Cleveland and Columbus, a committee of thirty "of all parties" tendered him a public dinner at the Commercial Exchange. According to a Cincinnati resident who attended the affair (June 19) Webster said there was "a deep settled determination" among southern politicians to produce a separation, which would have momentous consequences if it succeeded. He had declared that the President and his advisers deserved the everlasting gratitude of their country for promptly counteracting nullification. Webster also supported all internal improvements intended to advance western interests. He closed with the highest praise for the West in general and for Cincinnati in particular. "He said that there was nothing in all history to compare with our progress. . . . He had witnessed realities which more than equaled his highest expectations."[48]

Webster's address adroitly combined an appeal to the nationalism of the West with an appeal to its pocketbook and its sectional pride. The Cincinnati *Gazette* thought the speech "well conceived and happy—natural in all its aspects—a little flattering to the whole west—a little more so to Cincinnati in particular—and yet, perhaps, nothing short of the whole truth."[49]

A correspondent of the *United States Telegraph* reported from Cincinnati on June 18, that Webster was there "gladdening all hearts. Tomorrow he partakes of a public dinner, in which all parties unite, but in which the Jackson party have taken the lead. Their enthusiasm has been as great as ours."[50] William Barry, Jackson's Postmaster General, wrote Martin Van Buren that Webster had been "treated very kindly" in Cincinnati; "it was owing to the friends of Genl. Jackson that he was. . . . Mr. Clay's friends & especially his bank friends were cold, and dissatisfied with the speech of Mr. Webster at the dinner. It was a patriotic effort, in which the present administration was highly complimented."[51]

Under such circumstances, a visit to Henry Clay at Lexington might have proved extremely embarrassing to Webster. The Kentuckian would undoubtedly have questioned him sharply about his political bundling with the Democrats. However, when Webster reached Ohio, he learned that a cholera epidemic was raging in Kentucky; and this provided an excuse to avoid a meeting. On June 20, Webster left Cincinnati for the East. From Chillicothe, Ohio, where he spent two days with Duncan McArthur and other friends, he wrote to Clay to express his regret that he had not been able to visit him. "I found it unavoidable that I should give up the Kentucky portion of my journey"; he explained, "since, even though I felt no fear about personal safety, I should yet find those whom I wished to see either in alarm or in affliction. . . ."[52]

At Pittsburgh, on July 9, citizens invited him to a public collation in a grove outside the city. Webster delivered an address which represented his chief oratorical effort to conciliate the Jackson party. He stressed his support of Jackson's nullification policy, and confessed that the President's proclamation of December 10, 1832, had inspired him with new hopes for the duration of the Republic. Although he admitted that he had differed with the President upon many important subjects, "when the crisis arrived in which our constitution was in danger," he had felt himself bound to yield, "not a lame and hesitating, but a cordial and efficient support to his measures." Webster hoped Jackson might "go through with his administration and come out with as much success and glory as any of his predecessors. (*Great Applause*)."

Pittsburgh was a growing industrial center, and Webster extolled the merits of protection to an appreciative audience. Next to the Constitution itself, he declared, there was no more important question. A protective tariff was necessary to save American workers from English pauper labor, and for this reason he maintained the policy of the American System. The tariff would not be yielded without the severest struggle, and in this fight the interests of New England and Pennsylvania were identical. In conclusion, Webster again approved generous government aid to western internal improvements, including those most beneficial to Pittsburgh—the Ohio Canal, and the Baltimore and Ohio railroad.[53]

Webster considered this speech of such importance that he carefully revised the stenographer's notes and published the revision both in the newspapers and as a pamphlet.[54] He distributed copies to friends, and Richard Rush of Philadelphia sent him the following note: "I beg to thank you for the copy of your address to the citizens of Pittsburgh that you were kind enough to send me. I have just read it, and find it full of patriotism, good sense, good taste, and every kind of good feeling."[55] Webster's additions to the stenographer's account of the address were uniformly favorable to Jackson and to his own role in the nullification crisis. He obviously wanted his remarks to receive the widest possible circulation among members of the Jackson party.

Leaving Pittsburgh, Webster traveled to Baltimore. *Niles' Weekly Register*, published in that city, reported that he "seemed most gratified with the generous and kind attentions which had every where been paid to him, and by persons of every political party."[56]

The press lauded Webster's western tour. The Washington *Globe* declared that the "signal honor, with which Mr. W. has been received in different sections of the country, evinces the new feeling which has arisen in his favor, in consequence of the stand he took last winter in support of the principles of the Union. . . ." The Louisville *Journal* noted the friendliness of the Democrats: "Wherever he goes, the friends of the administration are peculiarly zealous to do him honor. The very men who, a year ago, were daily denouncing him as a Hartford convention traitor and the corrupt hireling of the Bank are now proud of the privilege of touching but the hem of his garment." "Mr. Webster has wrought little less than a miracle upon party feuds and division in the western country," the *National Intelligencer* gushed. "He has fairly extinguished the one and obliterated the other."[57]

One section of the administration press, however, implacably opposed a Jackson-Webster coalition. Isaac Hill's *New Hampshire Patriot* used the cry of "Federalist" to deter any member of the Democratic party who favored a union with Webster. ". . . far from discountenancing the Hartford Convention," the *Patriot* charged, "he was one of the *contrivers* of the plot, and the master spirit in this State [New Hampshire] to carry into effect its objects and purposes." The paper sneered that the story of a possible understanding between Webster and Jackson was "a weak device of the enemy." The Albany *Argus* also scouted all rumors of a coalition. "We see no cause," it declared, "to change our views of his [Webster's] general political course; and surely none to court his political association."[58]

Noting these declarations by the *Patriot* and *Argus* that they wanted no connection with Webster, the *United States Telegraph* commented: "It would seem . . . that very different feelings are entertained towards Mr. Webster by the democracy of the west and those of the north and east. . . . The *Patriot* and those it influences, are ultra-anti. The west are quite enthusiastic the other way. . . ."[59]

While Webster toured the West, Jackson, accompanied by Martin Van Buren, Levi Woodbury, Andrew Jackson Donelson, and Isaac Hill visited New England. The announcement of the President's intended visit created alarm among Democratic leaders in the Northeast, who feared he might become too friendly with Websterites. The *New Hampshire Patriot* declared that if "the President's visit is to produce such a state of things as did the visit of Mr. Monroe—if it is to result in *conciliating* his opponents and *discarding* his old friends, much as we desire to see him, we had rather he would not come at all."[60] Such ungracious sentiments brought a sharp rebuke from the Washington *Globe*. "If Massachusetts through her legislature deems it proper to mark the visit of the President to that State with any token of personal respect," it declared, "we should consider an attempt, on the part of those assuming to be exclusive party friends, to repel such kind intentions upon the ground that they proceed from political opponents, not only as illiberal to those proffering the courtesy, but derogatory to the object of it."[61]

National Republican newspapers interpreted Van Buren's presence in Jackson's party as a move to strengthen his support among New England Democrats, but D. G. Ogden wrote to Webster that his real motive was to watch Jackson in order to prevent any attempt upon the part of the Federalists "to coax and cajol the president."[62]

At this time, Seba Smith, editor of the Portland *Courier*, was authoring a series of humorous letters, supposedly written by a close friend of the President, one "Major Jack Downing." One letter, dealing with Jackson's New England tour, shrewdly satirized the dissension within Jackson's inner circle.

> There is some trouble among us here [Washington] a little, to know how we shall get along among the Federalists when we come that way. They say the Federalists in Massachusetts want to keep the President all to themselves when he comes there. But Mr. Van Buren says that'll never do; he must stick to the Democratic [sic] party; . . . Mr. McLane and Mr. Livingston advise him t'other way. They tell him he'd better treat the Federalists pretty civil, and shake hands with Daniel Webster. . . . And when they give this advice Mr. Lewis and Mr. Kendle hop right up mad as March hairs [sic], and tell him if he shakes hands with a single Federalist . . . the Democratic party will be ruined.[63]

Jackson arrived in Boston on June 21, and the next day Governor Levi Lincoln and other dignitaries warmly received him at the State House. Later Harvard University awarded the President an honorary Doctor of Law degree, much to the disgust of ex-President John Quincy Adams, who thought it a disgrace that his Alma Mater should confer "her highest literary honors upon a barbarian who could not write a sentence of grammar and hardly could spell his own name." However, President Josiah Quincy, senior, of Harvard told Adams that Monroe had been awarded a degree in 1817 and "that the omission to show the same respect to President Jackson . . . would be imputed to party spirit—which they were anxious to avoid." When Jackson was forced to cut short his visit because of severe illness, Adams commented sourly in his diary: "The President must hasten back to Washington, or he will be glorified into his grave."[64]

P. P. F. Degrand wrote to Nicholas Biddle from Boston that Jackson's reception in Massachusetts had been chiefly the work of Webster's friends. Stephen White had quit Webster's western tour to serve as chairman of the legislative committee appointed to receive the President. Jackson had been welcomed as the "Defender of N. O. [New Orleans]" and as one who had expressed New England's principles in his proclamation of December 10. Moreover, said Degrand:

> Jackson is very much pleased, with his visit, to this quarter & grateful for these attentions & *quite gratified* that his "Union must be preserved" is fully sustained here. . . . In fact, it cannot be denied that a sympathy is excited, in his breast & between him & those who approached him here & that this sympathy pervades both.

It was evident, Degrand concluded, that Webster no longer supported Clay, but stood forth as "the Defender of the Constitution" (i.e. of the Administration), "while 'the Admn hold the Proclamation, as their standard.' " He would not be surprised if "with a view to weaken Clay, in the West & extreme South, the Jackson Party were willing to give Webster a degree of currency there, not sufficient, however (in their opinion) to out do Van Buren."[65]

Not all Webster's friends looked with favor upon the idea of a coalition with Jackson. Rufus Choate advised Webster that he had attended a National Republican dinner in Essex on July 4, the specific and immediate object of which "was to keep our own ranks; & to see that none of our numbers were carried away by the recent flow of good feeling." He warned Webster that "our Jackson men here are Van Buren men." The object of the Democratic party was to elect Van Buren President, and it was the business of the National Republicans to hang together and prevent it.[66]

Shortly after Jackson's visit to New England, Webster met Edward Livingston for their long delayed conference. This meeting may have taken place aboard a boat sailing from Philadelphia to New York City on July 18, 1833. Although the initiative for the meeting came from Webster and Biddle, Livingston was anxious to secure the Senator's adherence to the Jackson administration, and he repeated to Webster the substance of "frequent conversations" with Jackson on this subject. Friends of Webster believed at the time that a cabinet post was tendered to him at the meeting, but this was doubtful.[67]

While no concrete results were discernible from the Webster-Livingston talk, Webster's friends were promoting a realignment of parties by other means. On July 4, 1833, a new paper, *The Examiner*, began publication in Washington, edited by Eli Davis, who had written Webster in March about starting a Unionist paper in the capital. Although no copy of the July 4 issue has come to light, the *United States Telegraph* of July 5 announced the establishment of the *Examiner* and noted that it had nominated Webster as a candidate for the presidency and pledged its support to the author of the anti-nullification doctrine.[68] On August 12, the *New Hampshire Patriot* commented editorially:

> *The new candidate for the Presidency.*—If we may give credit to sundry indications, *Daniel Webster* is in earnest in his intention to be a candidate for the Presidency at the next election. A new paper has been started at Washington called the *Examiner,* the first number of which nominates Mr. Webster; and it is said a bosom friend of the 'godlike' in Massachusetts foots the bills necessary to start the new establishment.[69]

In an editorial of August 22, Davis replied to what he termed an "unprovoked and scurrilous" attack by the *Patriot* in this and other editorials upon both Webster and the *Examiner*. He denied that he had nominated Webster for the presidency, since only the people could make such a nomination, but added that when they had acted, "as we have no doubt they *will* do," then his "feeble efforts" would be exerted to render the nomination effectual. The *Patriot* had also accused Webster of being a Federalist, but Davis confessed that he had never been able to distinguish the slightest shade of difference in the principles of the President's proclamation and those avowed and supported by Webster.

> Nothing in truth can be more absurd and ridiculous in the existing state of parties than the attempt to keep up the *names* that once designated the two great political divisions. Every landmark has been thrown down, there no longer exists a single point to mark the boundaries that once separated the two parties.

"Who have been Gen. Jackson's most prominent supporters?" asked Davis. "Those once known as federalists. Who have been among his most inveterate opposers and revilers? Those who attempt to gull the people with the name of *democrat*."[70]

It was clearly Davis' purpose to stress the similarity of Jackson's and Webster's unionism as a basis for denying the existence of old party distinctions. Implicit in his position was the belief that a new party should be formed on a Constitution and Union platform. This point of view was explicitly presented by two other papers friendly to Webster, the Philadelphia *National Gazette* and the Boston *Courier*.

Like the *Examiner,* the *National Gazette* denied the validity of the terms Federalism and Federal principles with regard to old party distinctions. Jackson's proclamation against nullification had utterly confounded all nominal distinctions, save the vital one of Unionists and nullifiers. It would be a mockery to cite Webster as a Federalist, as the *New Hampshire Patriot* was doing, in any other sense than that having originally held the creed now held by the greater part of the Union, "he is worthy of particular and chief reliance for the maintenance of it in the highest executive department." The *National Gazette* asserted that the main and serious distinction of American parties in the future would be "that of the *Unionists,* on the one hand . . . and, on the other, the disaffected Nullifiers and half-Nullifiers of the South. . . ."[71]

The Boston *Courier,* edited by an old Federalist, Joseph Tinker Buckingham, was perhaps the most devoted Webster organ in the nation; and it too took up the cudgels for a new Union party. In an August 8 editorial entitled "The Presidency—New Parties," Buckingham declared that the presidential canvass was opened in earnest and that a new organization of parties was not only desirable but necessary. The events of the past eight months had demonstrated that unless the prejudices and partialities which had kept men adhering to the fragments of parties could be overcome, the Union and the Constitution would both be overthrown. The time for action had therefore come:

> Let the principles of the President's proclamation be the principles on which to raise up this new organization. . . . Let the *advocates* of those principles . . . give up all other differences of opinion—let us have no Jacksonians nor National Republicans, as party men—let us have no Freemasons nor Antimasons, no Southrons nor Northmen—but let all be for the principles of the Proclamation, and let the watchword be Union and the Constitution.[72]

Henry A. Dearborn, a former member of the House of Representatives, prepared a circular letter for distribution among political leaders throughout the country urging Webster's nomination on a Constitution and Union platform. He sent the Senator a draft with the request that he furnish additional names, if any, for the mailing list. Dearborn stated that he was enclosing a copy of the Boston *Courier* editorial of August 8 with each letter.[73]

In the letter, Dearborn said the presidential canvass had opened, and the friends of the Constitution and the Union must decide on a candidate who could gain the votes of all those, of whatever previous party, anxious to perpetuate the Union "upon the prosperity of the *Whole People.*" From all indications, Webster was "the candidate who will rally the most powerful party under the battle cry of '*The Constitution & the Union.*'" The *Courier* editorial indicated the views of National Republicans in Massachusetts. Dearborn requested information as to local public opinion on this "momentous subject" and on the course to be pursued in furthering Webster's candidacy.[74]

To counter the Democratic charge that he had been an active participant in the events leading to the Hartford Convention, Webster asked Edward Cutts of Portsmouth, New Hampshire, to secure documentary evidence that Webster had actively helped in preparing Portsmouth for defense against an expected British attack in 1814 and had not participated in the movement for the convention. After a long search, Cutts found the minutes of the Committee of Defense and transcribed most of its contents, "wherein your name is particularly connected." In a conversation with Captain William Rice, a member of the Committee, Rice remarked "that no man was more zealous or more heartily engaged in making preparations for the defence of the town than Mr. Webster and Mr. [Jeremiah] Mason." Cutts thought that a "very strong statement" about Webster's active and able part could doubtless be obtained from the surviving members of the Committee. However, Cutts could recall no conversation with Webster on the Hartford Convention, although he thought that when the calling of that meeting was first agitated, "you were in the western counties in this State & that immediately after your return to Portsmouth, you proceeded to Washington."[75]

That Webster would be a candidate for the presidency at the next election was generally acknowledged throughout the country. The Richmond *Whig* declared he was "filling a large space in the nation's eye"; and in the East and West, was rapidly superseding Van Buren as the "prominent Administration Presidential Candidate for those quarters." The Lynchburg *Virginian* thought it evident there was a strong and growing party in favor of his elevation to the presidency and predicted he would be brought out *"nolens volens."*[76] However, Webster said privately in October 1833 that while his friends in Ohio and Pennsylvania believed a nomination could be obtained from those states that would be entitled to great weight, he thought it too early for such action.[77]

In Washington, "Major Jack Downing" had a September morning conversation with Jackson in the East Room of the White House. The "Gineral" warned that the country was to see "a blacker storm of nullification, before many years come about, than ever it has seen yet"; and if there wasn't someone at the helm who knew how to steer pretty well, the old ship of state must go down. He himself was getting old, and must give up soon, and then what would become of her? He had been thinking that if Webster and the Major would put their heads together, and take charge of her until the storm had blown over, she might be saved from the jaws of nullification. "And I don't know who else can." This puzzled the Major:

> "But how do you mean, Gineral?" says I. "Why, to speak plain," says he, "if nullification shows its head, Daniel must talk and you must fight. There's nothing else will do the job for it that I know of. Daniel must go into the Presidential chair, and you must take command of the army, and then things will go straight."

Downing is a "little struck up" at this, and remonstrates with Jackson that "Daniel" is a Federalist, a Hartford Convention Federalist, and were the jaws of nullification worse than those of Federalism? At this, the President "starts up" and throws his cigar out of the window. "But how do you know, Major Downing, that Daniel is a Federalist?" he asks.

> "Because," say I, "I've heard him called so Down East more than a hundred times." "And that's just all you know about it," says he. "Now, I tell you how 'tis, Major Downing, Daniel is as thorough a Republican as you be, or as I be, and has been ever since my proclamation came out against nullification. As soon as that proclamation came out, Daniel came right over on to Republican ground, and took it upon his shoulder, and carried it through thick and thin, where no other man in the country could have carried it." Says I, "Gineral, is that a fact?" And says he, "Yes, you may depend upon it, 'tis every word truth."[78]

Political humor, to be effective, must cut close to the bone. Seba Smith's facile pen had neatly skewered the Websterite muddling of party distinctions. In a more serious vein, John W. Taylor of New York, a former speaker of the House, reported to Judge McLean that "the Eastern friends of Mr. Webster think a successful rally under him is not desperate."[79] Certainly there was every indication this was their intention. Webster's correspondence with Unionist leaders in the South, his western tour, Jackson's warm reception by Webster's friends in Massachusetts, the establishment of the Washington *Examiner*, Webster's negotiations with Edward Livingston, the editorial policy of the Philadelphia *National Gazette* and Boston *Courier,* and Dearborn's circular letter, all looked to the formation of a Constitution and Union party with Webster at its head. Unfortunately, a prime requisite for a realignment of parties—the peaceful settlement of the Bank question—had not been accomplished by September 1833. Jackson's hostility to the institution had not been removed or even mitigated. If he should order the removal of the government deposits from the Bank, as he had been threatening to do for some months, a formation of parties on the "union" issue would be rendered still more difficult if not impossible.

## NOTES

*1.* Amos Kendall to Martin Van Buren, November 2, 1832, Martin Van Buren Papers, Manuscript Division, Library of Congress. (Hereafter cited as Van Buren Papers.)

*2.* Carroll, *Whig Party,* pp. 80-81, quoting the Salem *Gazette,* [March, 1833].

*3.* P. P. F. Degrand to Nicholas Biddle, February 15, 1833, Biddle Papers.

*4.* William O. Lynch, *Fifty Years of Party Warfare, 1789-1837* (Indianapolis, 1931), pp. 440, 452-453.

*5.* Davis to Daniel Webster, March 27, 1833, Webster Papers.

*6.* Bryson to Eli Davis, April 1, 1833, *ibid.*

*7.* Clay to Nicholas Biddle, April 10, 1833, *Biddle Correspondence,* p. 203.

*8.* Fitzpatrick, "Autobiography," pp. 687-688.

*9.* Sprague to Henry Clay, March 19, 1833, *Clay Correspondence,* pp. 354-355; Clay to Nicholas Biddle, April 10, 1833, *Biddle Correspondence,* p. 203.

*10.* Concord *New Hampshire Patriot,* February 18, 1833.

*11.* Albany *Argus,* March 8, 1833.

*12.* Current, *Daniel Webster,* p. 80.

*13.* Kendall to Martin Van Buren, November 10, 1832, Van Buren Papers.

*14.* Philadelphia *National Gazette,* March 30, 1833; Washington *Globe,* March 29, 1833.

*15.* Jackson to John Coffee, April 9, 1833, *Jackson Correspondence,* V, 56.

*16.* Webster to Benjamin F. Perry, April 10, 1833, quoted in Curtis, *Life of Webster,* I, 158; Webster to Joel R. Poinsett, May 7, 1833, *Writings and Speeches,* XVI, 672-673.

*17.* Poinsett to Andrew Jackson, March 21, 1833, *Jackson Correspondence,* V, 45.

*18.* Poinsett to Daniel Webster, May 24, 1833, Webster Papers.

*19.* Philadelphia *National Gazette,* March 30, 1833. The editor of the *National Gazette* was Robert Walsh, of whom Clay acidly remarked that "he has but one God, and Mr. Webster is his prophet." Clay to J. S. Johnston, March 15, 1833, quoted in John Julius Reed, "The Emergence of the Whig Party in the North: Massachusetts, New York, Pennsylvania, and Ohio" (unpublished doctoral dissertation, University of Pennsylvania, 1953), p. 89.

*20.* Washington *Globe,* April 5, 1833.

*21.* Poinsett to Daniel Webster, May 24, 1833, Webster Papers.

*22.* Bolton to Daniel Webster, May 16, 1833, *Niles' Weekly Register,* XLIV (1833), 295, quoting Savannah *Georgian,* n.d.

*23.* Webster to John Bolton, May 17, 1833, *ibid.*

*24. Ibid.;* Washington *Globe,* July 4, 1833.

*25.* Quoted in Fuess, *Daniel Webster,* II, 4.

*26.* Washington *Globe,* April 23, 1833.

*27.* Jackson to Hardy M. Cryer, April 7, 1833, *Jackson Correspondence,* V, 53.

*28.* Ralph C. H. Catterall, *The Second Bank of the United States* (Chicago, 1903), p. 290.

*29.* Biddle to Henry Clay, March 25, 1833, *Clay Correspondence,* pp. 356-357.

*30.* Webster to Nicholas Biddle, April 7, 1833, Biddle Papers.

*31.* Biddle to Daniel Webster, April 8, 1833, *Biddle Correspondence,* p. 202; Biddle to Daniel Webster, April 10, 1833, Biddle Papers.

*32.* Webster to Edward Livingston [March 21, 1833], *Writings and Speeches,* XVI, 229-230.

*33.* Webster to Nicholas Biddle, April 13, 20, 1833, Biddle Papers.

*34.* Webster to Nicholas Biddle [March-April, 1833], *ibid.*

*35.* Webster to Nicholas Biddle, April 8, 1833, *ibid.*

*36.* Webster to Nicholas Biddle, April 21, 1833, *ibid.*

*37.* McLane to James Buchanan, June 20, [1833], quoted in George Ticknor Curtis, *Life of James Buchanan, Fifteenth President of the United States* (New York, 1883), I, 191.

*38.* Lewis to James A. Hamilton, June 22, 1833, quoted in James A. Hamilton, *Reminiscences of James A. Hamilton; or, Men and Events, at Home and Abroad, During Three Quarters of a Century* (New York, 1869), p. 259.

*39.* Cass to Daniel Webster, April 17, 1833, quoted in Curtis, *Life of Webster,* I, 460-461.

*40.* Webster to Lewis Cass, undated, quoted in *ibid.,* p. 461.

*41.* Washington *National Intelligencer,* May 30, 1833, quoting Albany *Journal,* n.d.; Curtis, *Life of Webster,* I, 461-462.

*42.* Washington *National Intelligencer,* June 15, 1833, quoting New York *Commercial Advertiser,* n.d.; *Niles' Weekly Register,* XLIV (1833), 256-257.

*43.* Concord *New Hampshire Patriot,* July 29, 1833. Shortly before departing on his western trip, Webster drew up a list of "Objects" which he intended to pursue in the coming months. He was determined to maintain the Union and the Constitution against nullification, to support the Administration in all its "just & proper measures," to "cherish a sympathy of feeling & encourage cooperation in action, with the friends of Union & Liberty in the South," to work for a recharter of the Bank of the United States, to maintain the protective tariff, and to oppose all secret organizations. *Letters of Webster,* p. 183.

*44.* Tracy to Thurlow Weed, June 10, 1833, quoted in Thurlow Weed Barnes, *Memoir of Thurlow Weed* (Boston, 1884), p. 49. Oran Follett, National Republican editor of the Buffalo *Daily Journal,* reported the same day that Tracy, "at the head of antimasonry amongst us," was preparing himself for some move. "The truth is, the Antis came near running clear off with the god-like Daniel. We would not permit this for the plain reason that we could drop him ourselves much easier than we could force them to do it." Oran Follett to William Larned Marcy, June 10, 1833, in L. B. Hamlin (ed.), "Selections from the Follett Papers, IV," *Quarterly Publication of the Historical and Philosophical Society of Ohio,* XI (1916), 9.

*45.* For a perceptive analysis of Webster's pro-western views see Peter J. Parish, "Daniel Webster, New England, and the West," *Journal of American History,* LIV (1967), 524-549.

*46.* Washington *National Intelligencer,* June 25, 1833.

*47.* Carroll, *Whig Party,* quoting Louisville *Journal,* n.d.

*48.* Philadelphia *National Gazette,* June 26, 1833.

*49.* *Niles' Weekly Register,* XLIV (1833), 317-318, quoting Cincinnati *Gazette,* June 21, 1833.

*50.* Washington *United States Telegraph,* July 8, 1833.

*51.* Barry to Martin Van Buren, July 7, 1833, Van Buren Papers.

*52.* Webster to Henry Clay, June 22, 1833, *Writings and Speeches,* XVI, 231-232.

*53.* *Niles' Weekly Register,* XLIV (1833), 362-364. This summary of Webster's address is taken from the stenographic notes of T. C. Gould, who was present at the collation for this purpose.

*54.* Washington *National Intelligencer,* September 25, 1833; *Niles' Weekly Register,* XLV (1833), 108-109; Daniel Webster, *Address to the Citizens of Pittsburgh, July 9, 1833* (Boston, 1833).

*55.* Rush to Daniel Webster, September 30, 1833, Webster Papers.

*56.* *Niles' Weekly Register,* XLIV (1833), 338.

*57.* Washington *Globe,* June 25, 1833; Carroll, *Whig Party,* p. 93, quoting Louisville *Journal,* n.d.; Washington *National Intelligencer,* July 11, 1833.

*58.* Concord *New Hampshire Patriot,* July 15, 29, 1833; Albany *Argus,* July 12, 1833.

*59.* Washington *United States Telegraph,* July 15, 1833.

*60.* Concord *New Hampshire Patriot,* May 5, 1833.

*61.* Washington *Globe,* April 23, 1833.

*62.* Ogden to Daniel Webster, April 27, 1833, quoted in Carroll, *Whig Party,* p. 90.

*63.* [Seba Smith], *My Thirty Years Out of the Senate, By Major Jack Downing* (New York, 1859), p. 201.

*64.* Adams, *Memoirs,* VIII, 546-547, IX, 4.

*65.* Degrand to Nicholas Biddle, July 4, 1833, Biddle Papers. In a postscript Degrand reported that Stephen White had attended the "True Blue Jackson Celebration" at Noddle's Island on July 4, where he had given a toast about the "Era of Good Feelings." "Observe—," Degrand concluded, *"Jackson* is kindly recd at the *East 'without distinction of party';*—&, at the same time, *Webster* is kindly recd, *at the West, without distinction of Parties."*

*66.* Choate to Daniel Webster, August 12, 1833, *Letters of Webster,* p. 184.

*67.* Philadelphia *National Gazette,* July 19, 1833; Hatcher, *Edward Livingston,* pp. 393-394; March, *Webster and His Contemporaries,* pp. 249-251; Curtis, *Life of Webster,* I, 464.

*68.* Washington *United States Telegraph,* July 5, 1833.

*69.* Concord *New Hampshire Patriot,* August 12, 1833.

*70.* Washington *Examiner,* August 22, 1833. The *Examiner* ceased publication sometime in the fall or early winter of 1833. The last known issue is September 5, 1833.

*71.* Philadelphia *National Gazette,* July 27, 1833.

*72.* Boston *Courier,* August 8, 1833.

*73.* Dearborn to Daniel Webster, August 12, 1833, *Letters of Webster,* p. 185.

*74. Ibid.,* pp. 185-186.

*75.* Cutts to Daniel Webster, August 23, 1833, Webster Papers.

*76.* Philadelphia *National Gazette,* July 27, 1833, quoting Richmond *Whig,* n.d.; *ibid.,* quoting Lynchburg *Virginian,* n.d. See also Concord *New Hampshire Patriot,* August 5, 12, 1833.

*77.* Plumer, "Reminiscences of Daniel Webster," *Writings and Speeches,* XVII, 557-558.

*78.* Smith, *My Thirty Years Out of the Senate,* pp. 238-242.

*79.* Taylor to John McLean, September 19, 1833, quoted in Reed, "Emergence of the Whig Party in the North," p. 76.

# WEBSTER JOINS THE CLAY-CALHOUN COALITION

4 In his efforts to reach an understanding with Andrew Jackson, Webster had enjoyed the discreet support of Nicholas Biddle, who hoped to influence the President through the Bank's great champion. But Jackson, even in the midst of his triumphant New England tour, contemplated a final crippling blow against "The Monster." He wrote William Duane, the new Secretary of the Treasury from Boston, that on September 15, 1833, "at the furthest," the government should discontinue deposits in the Bank and draw upon the balance to meet ordinary expenses.[1] On September 18, Jackson read a paper to the cabinet outlining his reasons for removing the deposits. When Duane refused to carry out this policy, he was dismissed and Attorney-General Roger B. Taney took his place. On September 26, Taney issued the necessary order to remove the deposits. The Treasury continued drawing on its balance in the Bank to meet current expenses, but it now deposited new revenues in friendly state banks, called "pets" by the President's critics.

With Taney's order, the uneasy truce in the Bank war came to an end. Biddle now lost interest in a Webster-Jackson coalition and sought instead to organize an anti-Jackson, pro-bank party for the next session of Congress. The olive branch having failed, he would try the bludgeon. He began calling in the Bank's loans and restricting its discount of notes. This policy of contraction, at its beginning, was thoroughly justified, since no one could predict what further action Jackson might take to destroy the Bank. But Biddle continued the contraction into the winter and spring of 1833-1834, when it was no longer necessary to safeguard the Bank. He believed that the general distress occasioned by loan curtailment would create a demand for recharter in the business community that would prove irresistible.[2]

Biddle counted upon Webster's assistance, but the Senator was loath to join Clay and Calhoun without one last effort to reach an understanding with the President. No reconciliation had been made with Clay and when the Kentuckian paid a fence mending visit to New England in October, Webster's friends did not participate in the Boston reception.[3] The *New Hampshire Patriot,* noting this coolness and the absence of Webster's name from the proceedings, queried: "Is Mr. Webster fearful that Mr. Clay will refuse to surrender the field to him at the next canvass for President, or has he really made up his mind to come over to the President?" "The coldness manifested towards Mr. Clay is ominous," declared the *Patriot.* "We shall see how the 'godlike' will play his hand this winter."[4]

William Plumer visited Webster after the removal of the deposits and thought he intended to pursue a more independent course at the next session of Congress.[5] A letter from Stephen White to Webster, written in January 1834, bore out this supposition:

. . . your resolution had been made up not to arouse, if possible, in the course you should adopt in the Senate, any opposition on mere party or local grounds to the measures of the administration: that the opinions and measures of the nullifiers were of so dangerous and monstrous a character that the preservation of the union and the maintenance of the legitimate powers of the general government were with you paramount objects . . . moderation and a conciliatory course would have secured the support of many powerful and patriotic minds.[6]

Biddle had no inkling of Webster's further pursuit of presidential favor. When the Twenty-third Congress assembled in December 1833, he sent Webster two copies of a short memorial from the directors of the Bank to the Senate and House of Representatives, protesting against the removal of the deposits as a violation of the chartered rights of the stockholders and asking "such redress therefore as to your sense of justice may seem proper." Biddle asked Webster to consult with Representative Horace Binney as to the most appropriate time and manner of presenting them—"doing exactly as you & he may deem most advantageous."[7]

Webster first disclosed his new independence on December 12, as the Senate prepared to select members of its committees. Felix Grundy, a Jackson senator from Tennessee, suddenly moved that selection of committees be postponed until Monday, December 16, 1833, assigning as reasons the absence of several senators. Clay, acting as floor leader of the anti-Jackson party, opposed this motion since he expected to control the appointments in a manner favorable to the Bank's interest. To his obvious astonishment, Webster suddenly rose and burst a bombshell in the ranks of the Bank forces. He announced his support for Grundy's motion and presented arguments for its passage almost identical to those put forward by the Tennessee senator. In disbelief, Clay questioned Webster sharply:

CLAY. I understand the gentleman to say it is time to proceed to the appointment of committees.
WEBSTER. I said it was an early period to take up important business.
CLAY. At no time, I believe, has the appointment of committees been delayed beyond the second week of the session.[8]

When it was voted upon, Grundy's motion passed twenty-eight to thirteen, with Webster and nine other opposition senators, including seven from New England, voting with the administration against Clay and Calhoun. Stunned, the Bank forces secured a Senate adjournment until the new time set for the voting, December 16.[9] With Webster's defection, there was a definite possibility that the selection of committees would be controlled by the administration. Clay, alarmed, hastily wrote to Senator John M. Clayton of Delaware, who had not yet left home.

> Until today, we have gone on swimmingly in the Senate. On Tuesday last this day was assigned to proceed to the appointment of the committees by the Senate itself. We came prepared . . . to carry them, if all proved faithful. To my surprise a motion was made by Mr. Grundy and supported by *Mr. Webster* to postpone the appointment until Monday next and it was carried. If you are here, I believe we shall be safe, even if there be defection. For God's sake then come to us. And do not let anything keep you away.[10]

Webster's unexpected action created "astonishment and suspicion" among Jackson's opponents in Washington. A correspondent of the Franklin (Mass.) *Mercury* reported that some "believe or affect to believe that these things are precursors of an alliance with Van Buren; others with greater plausibility find in them merely the symptoms of a determination to separate from Clay, and lead a third party, which shall give an occasional support to the administration without committing itself to any side." The writer did not find it singular that Webster resented Clay's superior personal influence: "Each is better fitted to command than obey, and each might look in vain for a rival till he found one in the other." In any event, another week would determine the truth or falsehood of these surmises. One thing was certain; "if Jackson committees are appointed, and Jackson influence predominates in the Senate, it will be through Mr. Webster's influence alone."[11]

Martin Van Buren reached Washington on Saturday, December 14, and the next day was summoned to an early morning meeting at the White House. Arriving there, Van Buren found

Jackson and Grundy awaiting him with a startling proposal and learned for the first time why the appointment of committees had been postponed:

> Mr. Grundy then spoke of the probable character of the session, the exciting nature of the subjects that would require action and of the importance to the administration of having the committees as favorably constituted as possible. . . . He had, he said, what he considered sufficient reason to believe that an arrangement could be made with Mr. Webster and his friends by which the latter object could be materially promoted. He had expressed that opinion to the President by whom he had been informed of the time when I would reach Washington and requested that no step should be taken in the matter before I had been consulted; hence the postponement of the choice of committees and the application for the present interview.[12]

Van Buren did not stop to ask Grundy the reasons for his belief in the practicability of his proposal, but immediately launched a sharp attack upon it, pointing out the antagonistic positions which Webster and Jackson had always occupied on the Bank, the evil effect of such an alliance on public opinion, and the political ammunition it would furnish Clay. He knew troubles were ahead, the certain severity of the struggle, but declared he was prepared for it "and would enter upon it in the full conviction that the people, if nothing occurred to blunt their ardour or to raise a doubt of the purity and disinterestedness of the General's aims, in which they now implicitly confided, would carry us, as on many previous occasions they had carried us, triumphantly thro' the crisis." This was a shrewd argument, for Jackson prided himself on his popularity with the people. The three men had remained standing throughout the interview—the President resting his hand upon the mantle. When Van Buren finished, Jackson turned to Grundy, who had made no response, and advised him to drop the matter, to which the latter assented and immediately withdrew. According to Van Buren, "between neither of these gentlemen and myself was the subject ever revived."[13]

Rebuffed by the President, Webster and his friends had no choice but to align themselves with Clay and Calhoun in the appointment of committees; and Webster himself, as a gesture of appeasement after his attempted bolt, was selected as chairman of the important Finance Committee. Indeed, he fairly forced Clay to give him the chairmanship of this committee as the price of his continued support. "Webster has been on the point of desertion to the admn.—*There is no mistake in this,*" Senator Willie P. Mangum confided to a friend. "—He insisted upon displacing Clay from the head of the Finance Commee.—The whole admn. force wd. have gone for him agt. Clay—and three or four other votes, his own included—Clay, I think, weakly yielded—He says now, that he fears his friend Mr. W. has given himself a fatal stab among his own friends, but that now if 'he deserts, it will be with infamy.' "[14]

Biddle, learning of Webster's defection, had written him in alarm that "you three [Webster, Clay, and Calhoun] should not be alienated from each other," adding fretfully: "You can scarcely imagine how often and earnestly the few casual phrases which have passed between Mr. Clay and yourself have been criticized & weighed, one side in hope, & the other in fear, of finding something to indicate estrangement between you. For all our sakes, do not let this grow into any difficulty."[15] Webster replied that he was taking Biddle's "sermon" to heart and that there was "no coolness whatever" between the friends of the Bank. He admitted that "some little difficulties" had been found in arranging the Senate committees, but these had been overcome by "mutual & friendly arrangements."[16] Two days later, Webster's tone became surly and demanding. "Since I have arrived here, I have had an application to be concerned, professionally, against the Bank, which I have declined, of course, although I believe my retainer has not been renewed or *refreshed* as usual. If it be wished that my relation to the Bank should be continued, it may be well to send me the usual retainers."[17]

Although he needed the money, Webster assured Biddle in a private note that he need give no attention to the matter if he thought it more *"prudent"* to wait a while. "I shall not undertake, professionally, agt. the Bank, whether you answer this, or not—If such things have to go before the *Board,* I should prefer the subject should be *postponed.*"[18] Biddle did not send the requested retainer. To do so, he wrote, would be risky; within forty-eight hours the editor of the *Globe* would learn of the transaction. He could either publish the fact immediately or store it "to be used on the first occasion when any vote of yours gave displeasure to that gang." Biddle also suggested that the Senate refuse to confirm the renominations of John T. Sullivan, Henry Gilpin, and Peter Wager as government directors, since these men reported confidential business to Jackson. They were the ones "who watch your account and the account of every political antagonist . . . who take no share in the affairs of the Bank, except to report and misrepresent every transaction of every individual opposed to them. Depend upon it these people should be expelled now that you have the power."[19] The Senate eventually rejected all three and as soon as they left the board, Webster's legal retainer arrived in Washington.

For a time, Webster's friends urged neutrality as an alternative to surrender to the Clay-Calhoun coalition. Stephen White wrote from Boston that "the mad pranks of old Jackson under the influence of Cabinet impulses and of his old natural recklessness" had placed Webster in a difficult position. However, Webster should not commit himself upon important issues to either party. White reported that "the Jackson people here, the best class of them I mean, lament deeply the course taken by the General as tending to drive into opposition those whose talents and influence would have been a tower of strength to the administration."[20] Henry W. Conrad of Philadelphia, a "strong and decided friend" of Jackson's, assured Webster that his stand against nullification and his subsequent declarations on his western tour had made a deep and favorable impression on the Jackson party in Pennsylvania. Van Buren's hold on the state was tenuous and might be weakened by future events. "Therefore . . . do not think I attempt to mislead you when I say that the disinterested part of the Jackson party in our State are looking up to you, that they are watching your course this winter with the most intense anxiety—"[21]

Coinciding as it did with his own predilections, Webster heeded this advice and tried to play an independent role in the

Senate. He was not pleased with Biddle's acceptance of Clay's leadership. When the Kentuckian introduced his censure resolutions against Jackson for his violation of the Constitution and the laws in relation to the public revenue, Webster felt "deeply compromised" by this "premature" movement, and threatened to send back the Bank's memorial protesting against the removal of the deposits with the request that someone else present it.[22] He remained stubbornly silent through the early part of the session, refused to join in personal attacks on the President, and in daily conversation, "still talked of expediency and of not wasting ammunition."[23]

This temporizing at last aroused Biddle's ire. When Binney reported Webster's private suggestion that the Finance Committee "inquire into the causes and remedies of the present troubles," Biddle immediately replied that the suggestion was "very unwise" and begged Binney to dissuade him, if he did not already see its injurious tendency.[24] To Webster went a preemptory demand that he *make a speech*—one of your calm, solid, stern works, that crushes, like the block of your Quincy Granite, all that it falls on." "I want that Jackson & Taney & Benton & all these people should fall by your hand," Biddle said sternly. "I wish you to do it for my sake. I wish you to do it for your own. We are annoyed perpetually by the whispers of exhultation which pass among these miserable people that Mr. Webster is to come out for them. Only think now of Whitney's writing here that it is perfectly settled that you are to leave your friends and go over to that gang. I wish to see some fair occasion on which you can dispel this illusion and demolish the whole concern."[25]

Such a warning had its effect. Webster could not remain neutral indefinitely, for the removal of the deposits dealt his hopes of forming a new party a near fatal blow. The renewed Bank war deadened enthusiasm for the President among National Republicans; and a majority of those who had opposed Calhoun and his friends now saw the necessity of working with them against the greater menace of Jackson policies. "There is no longer immediate danger from Southern nullification," declared the Philadelphia *National Gazette*, which had earlier warned of just such a threat, "but that which is enthroned at Washington is instant, active and formidable to the highest degree." Calhoun and his followers were now desirable auxiliaries to combat "much more guilty offenders and leaguers against the constitution and the essential weal of the Union."[26]

By January 1834, Webster was moving reluctantly but definitely into the Clay-Calhoun camp. On January 9, John Tyler reported that the "great bellwether" from the Northeast appeared to be growing more and more determined to adhere to his old friends.[27] Biddle received assurances from Binney that Webster's purposes "are what you wish them to be," although the time and mode of accomplishing them were matters of which Webster himself would judge, "& I have no reason to doubt will judge rightly."[28] By February 10, Biddle, who had been following Webster's movements, "with great interest and anxiety," could now "see every day with great satisfaction that you are going on gloriously."[29] Webster's friends were soon denying that he had ever considered an alliance with Jackson. Thus Rufus Choate assured a friend, perhaps too vehemently to carry conviction, that to his *"certain* knowledge there was never for a moment a thought or a possibility of a union between Mr. Webster & the Regency & Anti-Bank—*never for a moment."*[30]

From the beginning of the session, Webster had disliked Biddle's restriction on credit. He had advised him through Horace Binney "that the Bank ought to reduce as slowly and moderately as they can—and occasionally to ease off—where it is requisite to prevent extreme suffering," but he had said nothing publicly. But when Biddle was forced by a committee from New York to suspend curtailments, Webster felt free to present a compromise proposal. "It strikes me at present," he wrote to Nathan Appleton, "that the thing most likely to be done, in season to stop the mischief, is to continue the present Bank 3 or 5 yrs, leaving Congress at liberty to make another after 1836."[31] On March 18, he introduced a bill providing for the return of the public deposits to the Bank on July 1, 1834, and for an extension of the charter beyond March 4, 1837, when Jackson would retire from the presidency. According to Thomas Hart Benton, Webster's bill was "the only one that stood the least chance of getting through the two Houses; and on that point he had private assurances of support from friends of the administration, if all the friends of the bank stood firm."[32]  When Biddle found he could not prevent Webster from introducing his plan, he gave it reluctant support, in order not to offend Webster and the Senator's strong group of friends in Philadelphia. Webster assured him that "if M.C and Mr. C. [Clay and Calhoun] would go along with us, we could carry the compromise Bill through the Senate by a strong *two-thirds* majority."[33]  Clay, however, would not accept anything less than a full twenty year charter, while Calhoun was adamant on one of twelve years. The Kentuckian advised Biddle to make no movement toward renewal of the charter or the establishment of a new bank. The Bank ought to be kept in the rear, the President's usurpation in front. "It is the usurpation which has convulsed the country," Clay wrote. "If we put it by and take up the Bank, we may and probably would divide about the terms of the charter, and finally do nothing leaving things as they are—In the other course the recharter will follow. The country will take care of that."[34]  In accordance with this opinion, Clay forced Webster to table his bill on March 25. The last faint chance for a recharter was now irrevocably lost. Clay was determined that none but he should lead.[35]

On March 28, the censure resolutions, their phraseology slightly softened, passed the Senate. Webster voted for both resolutions but he did so with great reluctance. In his speech on Jackson's formal protest message, he lamented:

> As an individual member of the Senate, it gives me great pain to be engaged in such a conflict with the executive government. . . . I ardently hoped that nothing might occur to place me . . . in an attitude of opposition. In all respects, and in every way, it would have been far more agreeable to me to find nothing in the measures of the executive government which I could not cheerfully support. The present occasion of differences has not been sought by me. It is thrust upon me, in opposition to strong opinions and wishes, on my part not concealed.[36]

Webster's failure to reach an understanding with Jackson during the session of 1833-1834 marked the end of any possibility of a realignment of political parties. Nullification had lost its importance as a national issue and most politicians were happy to drop it and again raise old and less embarrassing questions. Influential leaders in both the National Republican and Democratic parties—Clay, Van Buren, and Hill, to name the most prominent—effectively opposed a new alignment. Some of Webster's friends believed at the time, "that among the motives which actuated some persons in General Jackson's confidence, in fanning his hostility to the Bank of the United States, was that of bringing forward a question of great interest both to the public and the President, on which he would be sure to encounter Mr. Webster's opposition."[37] Yet Webster continued to court the administration *after* the removal of the deposits in September 1833; only after Jackson, acting on Van Buren's advice, rejected his overtures, did he reluctantly join the Clay-Calhoun coalition. Had the Senator formed a new party on a Constitution and Union platform, his chances for the presidency in 1836 would have increased. "Had the war on the Bank of the United States not intervened," the prominent journalist John W. Forney later wrote, "I have always believed that Daniel Webster would have been a leader, if not the leader, of the Democratic party."[38] A Constitution and Union party would have been pulled strongly toward nationalism, and might have countered state rights sentiments.[39] But the new Whig party that emerged in 1834 contained both state rights men and nationalists. It had no common principles except hatred of the Hero and his works; and was dedicated to only one clearly defined object—to "cleanse the Augean stables" by turning the Democrats out of the presidency.

## NOTES

*1.* Jackson to William J. Duane, June 26, 1833, *Jackson Correspondence*, V, 111-128.

*2.* "Nothing but the evidence of suffering abroad will produce any effect in Congress," Biddle wrote the president of the Boston branch. "Our only safety is in pursuing a steady course of firm restriction—and I have no doubt that such a course will ultimately lead to a restoration of the currency and the recharter of the Bank" (Biddle to William Appleton, January 27, 1834, *Biddle Correspondence*, pp. 219-220).

*3.* Van Deusen, *Henry Clay*, p. 272. According to Eber Malcolm Carroll, "A comparison between the names of those prominent in the reception of Jackson and Clay indicates that Webster's friends while actively participating in the first were not involved in the second" (Carroll, *Whig Party*, p. 101n).

*4.* Concord *New Hampshire Patriot*, November 4, 1833.

*5.* Plumer, "Reminiscences of Daniel Webster," *Writings and Speeches*, XVII, 557-558.

*6.* White to Daniel Webster, January 9, 1834, quoted in Carroll, *Whig Party*, pp. 112-113.

*7.* Biddle to Daniel Webster, December 9, 1833, President's Letter Book, Private, No. 5 B.U. S., Biddle Papers, Manuscript Division, Library of Congress. (Hereafter cited as President's Letter Book No. 5. B.U. S.)

*8. Congressional Globe*, 23rd Cong., 1st Sess., Washington, 1833, I, 23-24.

*9. Ibid.*, p. 24. Opposition senators voting with Webster were George Bibb, Kentucky; Theodore Frelinghuysen, New Jersey; Gideon Tomlinson and Nathan Smith, Connecticut; Nehemiah Knight and Asher Robbins, Rhode Island; Samuel Prentiss and Benjamin Smith, Vermont; and Nathaniel Silsbee, Massachusetts. Only two New England senators, Samuel Bell of New Hampshire and Peleg Sprague of Maine, voted against the motion.

*10.* Clay to John M. Clayton, December 12, 1833, John M. Clayton Papers, Manuscript Division, Library of Congress.

*11.* Boston *Courier*, December 25, 1833, quoting Franklin (Mass.) *Mercury*, n.d. Duff Green, editor of the *United States Telegraph*, wrote Biddle at this time: ". . . I fear that you will be destroyed by Webster. Of this you may be better advised but unless I am much deceived he has made his terms with VB [Van Buren]" (Green to Nicholas Biddle, December 16, 1833, Biddle Papers).

*12.* Fitzpatrick, "Autobiography," pp. 677-679.

*13. Ibid.*, pp. 678-679. In 1849 Clay told Van Buren that this account of the meeting with Grundy and Jackson explained to the Kentuckian for the first time the reason for Webster's failure to arrange terms with the Administration (*ibid.*, p. 672).

*14.* Mangum to David L. Swain, December 22, 1833, in Henry Thomas Shanks (ed.), *The Papers of Willie Person Mangum* (Raleigh, 1950-1956), II, 55-56. (Hereafter cited as *Mangum Papers*.)

*15.* Biddle to Daniel Webster, December 15, 1833, President's Letter Book No. 5. B.U. S.

*16.* Webster to Nicholas Biddle, December 19, 1833, Biddle Papers.

*17.* Webster to Nicholas Biddle, December 21, 1833, *Biddle Correspondence*, p. 218.

*18.* Webster to Nicholas Biddle [December 21, 1833], Biddle Papers.

*19.* Biddle to Daniel Webster, December 25, 1833, *ibid.*

*20.* White to Daniel Webster, December 27, 1833, quoted in Carroll, *Whig Party*, pp. 111-112.

*21.* Conrad to Daniel Webster, December 17, 1833, Webster Papers. See also William Smith to Daniel Webster, February 9, 1834, *ibid.*

22. John Q. Watmought to Nicholas Biddle, December 30, 1833, Biddle Papers.

*23.* John Q. Watmought to Nicholas Biddle, December 22, 1833, *ibid.* A North Carolina representative reported on January 5, 1834, that Webster "has been thus far silent in the Senate, and there is great trepidation among the ranks of Clay and Calhoun lest he may support the administration" (James Graham to William A. Graham, January 5, 1834, in Joseph Gregoire de Roulhac Hamilton (ed.), *The Papers of William Alexander Graham* [Raleigh, 1957-1961], I, 281).

*24.* Binney to Nicholas Biddle, January 6, 1834, Biddle Papers; Biddle to Horace Binney, January 8, 1834, President's Letter Book No. 5. B.U. S.

*25.* Biddle to Daniel Webster, January 8, 1834, President's Letter Book No. 5. B.U.S.

*26.* Philadelphia *National Gazette,* December 18, 30, 1833.

*27.* Tyler to Littleton W. Tazewell, January 9, 1834, quoted in Lyon Gardiner Tyler, *The Letters and Times of the Tylers* (Richmond, 1884), I, 483.

*28.* Horace Binney to Nicholas Biddle, January 12, 1834, Biddle Papers.

*29.* Biddle to Daniel Webster, February 10, 1834, President's Letter Book No. 5. B.U.S.

*30.* Choate to Warwick Palfrey, Jr., January 31, 1834, "Rufus Choate Letters," Essex Institute *Historical Collections,* LXIX (1933), 87.

*31.* Horace Binney to Nicholas Biddle, February 4, 1834, quoted in Catterall, *Second Bank of the United States,* pp. 331-332; Webster to Nathan Appleton, February 2, 1834, *Writings and Speeches,* XVI, 240.

*32.* Benton, *Thirty Years' View,* I, 433.

*33.* Thomas Payne Govan, *Nicholas Biddle, Nationalist and Public Banker, 1786-1844* (Chicago, 1959), p. 265; Biddle to Daniel Webster, March 15, 1834, President's Letter Book No. 5, B.U.S.; Catterall, *Second Bank of the United States,* p. 336.

*34.* Clay to Nicholas Biddle, February 2, 1834, Biddle Papers.

*35.* Catterall, *Second Bank of the United States,* p. 338.

*36. Writings and Speeches,* VII, 104.

*37.* Daniel Webster, *The Works of Daniel Webster* (Boston, 1851), I, cix-cx. The quotation is from Edward Everett's "Biographical Memoir of the Public Life of Daniel Webster" in the first volume of this edition.

*38.* John W. Forney, *Anecdotes of Public Men* (New York, 1873), p. 134.

*39.* The Philadelphia *National Gazette* had once seen great advantages for nationalist policies in a realignment of parties: "The Unionists (now in the great majority of the people) will have something more to do for the final triumph of their cause than to resist the theory and practice of nullification; it will be essential on their side, that the national defense and plans of internal improvement, and the establishments which secure an independent judiciary, a sound currency, abundant revenue, and a domestic supply of manufactures, should be preserved" (July 27, 1833).

# A CANDIDATE
# FOR THE
# PRESIDENCY

**5** It was evident to thoughtful men that the National Republican party was dying. "What is this thing called the National Republican party?" asked John Quincy Adams' son, Charles Francis, in September 1833, and answered contemptuously, "A matter of thread and patches."[1] The following November, his father commented in *his* diary that "there is at this time a breaking up of parties, which strangely tries the temper and the principles of men."[2] The failure of the Antimasons to establish a wider base of popular support outside of New England and the Middle States clearly indicated the necessity of a new party that could rally the anti-Jackson men into some kind of political order.

Such a coalition emerged in Congress in the spring of 1834. The new party adopted the name "Whig" because of its opposition to the "reign of King Andrew" and stigmatized the President's followers as "Tories."[3] Clay first used the term Whig in the Senate on April 14, 1834. To a nucleus of National Republicans, were added a majority of the Antimasons, state rights men critical of Jackson's handling of nullification, and business-minded Democrats who deserted the President on the Bank issue. Members of the party could be found in every class of American society, but its hard core in the North was the business and professional men of the flourishing towns and cities, as well as a respectable number of commercial farmers. Native laborers, fearful of competing with cheap immigrant labor, also joined.[4] In the South, urban commercial and banking interests controlled the Whig party, joined by a majority of the planters, who were dependent on banking and credit facilities.[5]

In the late winter of 1834, prominent congressional leaders of the State Rights and National Republican parties met together with the purpose of bringing the two major elements of the opposition into agreement on a long range program looking at least as far ahead as the presidential election of 1836. On March 8, for example, John Quincy Adams dined with John C. Calhoun at Dawson's. Also present were William C. Preston, the other South Carolina senator; senators Willie P. Mangum, of North Carolina; Samuel L. Southard, of New Jersey; Peleg Sprague, of Maine; and John H. Fulton, a member of the House from Virginia. After dinner, Senator Benjamin Watkins Leigh of Virginia came in, also three House members, Samuel McDowell Moore, of Virginia; Dixon H. Lewis, of Alabama; and Warren R. Davis, of South Carolina. "The company sat late at table," Adams wrote, "and the conversation was chiefly upon politics. The company are all at this time adversaries of the present administration— most of them were adversaries of the last." Three nights later, Adams attended a dinner at which Edward Everett, Nathaniel Silsbee, Benjamin Gorham, and Levi Lincoln, all of Massachusetts, were present, along with Clay, Calhoun, and Preston.[6] Apparently Webster was not involved in these discussions. He had not abandoned all hope of some accommodation with the President on the Bank, and was about to submit his compromise bill to the Senate. Did he fear to offend Jackson by intriguing too openly with Clay and Calhoun?

These meetings failed in their main intent. Calhoun, while willing to cooperate with the Whigs against the administration, scrupulously maintained his formal independence of the "Nationals," as he continued to call them, never attended any of their caucuses, nor was he appointed to any of the standing senatorial committees. "I am the partisan of no class, nor, let me add, of either political party," he said in a Senate speech. "I am neither of the opposition nor administration." "If there is to be Union against the administration, it must be Union on our own ground"; he wrote Francis W. Pickens, "but of such Union I have but little hope. We are as wide as the poles."[7] This refusal to submerge principle in politics was not general among the critics of Jackson. One of Justice McLean's Ohio friends wrote him: "Our Whig party is made up of such a 'mixed multitude of discordant materials' that it is enough to sicken anyone of having ought to do with it."[8]

In the absence of any common political creed, the election of one of their own men as President in 1836 was the party's chief cement. As keen old Harrison Gray Otis shrewdly observed: "The Whig party is a coalition of persons, brought together from the four ends of our earth, led by instinctive impulse, not merely by compact of leaders, & united . . . as yet in only one defined object—a change of men."[9] Fortunately for the Whigs, the two term tradition and failing health would bar the President from another canvass, and almost certain victory. "The gorgon head of Andrew Jackson is no longer in the field against us," exulted one youthful Whig. "The smoke of that New Orleans victory will no longer blear and blind the eyes of the American people. The magic of that word Hero will no longer silence the tones of patriotic opposition. The spell is already broken, the charm dissolves apace, the bonds of that fatal destiny are scattered, the people are awakening. . . ."[10] Against any other man in the Democratic party, Whig chances could not help but improve.

But Whigs had their problems. If the election of a president was the chief unifying force in the new party, it was, paradoxically, also the most disruptive. The Whig "tribe," with its diverse, even incongruous elements, had too many ambitious chiefs who wanted the highest office. "That contemptible bauble, the Presidency, is to separate those who, but for it, could save the country," complained Charles Hammond, fiery editor of the Cincinnati *Gazette*. "Mr. Clay, Mr. Calhoun, and Mr. Webster cannot act together. The movement of one is not supported by the others. As practical men it is worse than idle to deceive ourselves. Neither is willing to aid the other in doing anything that may cause him to be looked upon as a public benefactor."[11]

The earliest candidate actually in the field was Associate Justice John McLean of the United States Supreme Court. The Ohioan was a hardy perennial who, John Quincy Adams declared, thought "of nothing but the Presidency by day and dreams of nothing else by night." As early as December 1832, he had begun "angling" for a nomination.[12] McLean hoped to arouse a respectable number of former Jacksonians in his favor, and by thus offering the National Republicans a chance for victory, to cause them to support him. In the fall of 1833, the McLean movement began to make headway with his nomination by a meeting of workingmen in Baltimore on October 25. The Judge formally consented to be a candidate in March 1834. He declared against a national nominating convention as having "a direct tendency to place the whole political power of the country into the hands of a few individuals, and to deprive the people of a full and fair expression of their will," and recommended state nominations instead.[13]

Henry Clay was also interested in the nomination, although he was warned that his heavy defeat in 1832 would forbid his selection. "I will be plain with you in this communication," wrote Oran Follett, editor of the Buffalo *Daily Journal* and an influential leader in western New York. "I feel the force of what I say, and no one regrets the necessity more than I do, that compels me to say, you are not the man on whom the friends of the country can rely for the canvass of 1836. This is the secret conviction of the whole Nat. Repub. party, with perhaps a few exceptions."[14] The Kentuckian later stated his unwillingness to run unless the Whigs could unite behind him, but this stand was coupled with a very critical attitude toward the availability of other possible nominees. Despite his unpopularity in New England because of the compromise tariff of 1833 and his understanding with Calhoun, he commanded a loyal following through-out the country. Some of his friends insisted on clinging to him, and Clay did not discourage them. "Mr. Clay does nothing, and will do nothing, at present," Webster grumbled to Jeremiah Mason in February 1835. "He thinks—or perhaps it is his friends who think—that *something* may yet occur, perhaps a war, which may, in *some* way, cause a general rally around him."[15]

Calhoun, meanwhile, continued to hold himself stubbornly aloof from the "Nationals." To Lewis S. Coryell, he wrote from his home, Fort Hill, on August 10, 1834, that the State Rights party of the South would rally on no man in the next presidential election who did not openly avow and support their doctrines. The "true policy" of the party was to stand fast on their principles, whether they rose or fell. If the administration party succeeded in New York in the November elections, the Nationals would receive their death blow, and the struggle would be between the administration party and the State Rights; but on the other hand, should the administration be defeated, "their party would aim their final blow," and the contest would be between the Nationals and the State Rights party. In neither event, in Calhoun's opin-ion, could McLean be formidable. "His position on the bench is bad for a candidate and the position taken by his friends not sufficiently well defined. He has no strength in the South." The State Rights party must ultimately rally on some other "party" (Calhoun?) and on more distinct ground. Calhoun's advice to his friends everywhere was to contend under their own colors. "It is the manly course; and as we have truth on our side, it must succeed. The South will soon be unanimous, and experience has shown that when united they cannot be defeated."[16]

Webster too hoped to grasp the glittering prize. His col-league, Senator Nathaniel Silsbee, told John Quincy Adams that Webster, to his certain knowledge, "indulged not only the hope but the expectation of being a successful candidate for the Presi-dency at the ensuing election."[17] His support of the Proclamation and the Force Bill had strengthened him in the North and made him the logical candidate of nationalists in that area. J. H. Ostrom of Utica, New York, wrote to Webster that he would support any candidate who held sound constitutional views and was not a nullifier. "If you have personally any views or interest to serve in this matter you ought to lose no time in letting your friends know it," he advised. "I would be happy to throw my public efforts and influence into the scale for your advancement."[18]

Before the close of the session of 1833-1834, Webster was enlisting support among the wealthy lawyers and merchants of New York City. On March 7, he beckoned the former mayor of that city, the aristocratic merchant, Philip Hone, into one of the Senate committee-rooms, where the two men had an hour's talk. "He unburdened his mind fully on the state of affairs and future prospects," Hone wrote in his diary that evening, "explained all that has passed, and fully laid open his future plans." Webster would be in New York in about two weeks, for one night, and wished Hone to convene a few political friends to meet and consult with him. The Senator showed Hone his compromise bank bill, and explained his views and expectations in relation to it. "I was exceedingly flattered by this mark of Mr. Webster's confidence, and certainly never heard a man talk so."[19]

Webster arrived at Hone's at four o'clock on April 2, and found David B. Ogden, Samuel Ward, James G. King, and others waiting to see him. Clay called the meeting a plan "to bring out Mr. Webster as a candidate for the Presidency." "We had a full, free, and interesting conversation," recorded Hone, "in which the great Massachusetts senator detailed all his operations during the session, and confirmed in the most emphatic manner the declaration which he had made to me at Washington, that the hopes of our friends there to bring about a favourable change in the affairs of the country rely mainly upon the success of the great struggle which is to take place in New York next week [election for mayor and charter officers]."[20] Having flattered these influential men by his candor, Webster left for Boston the next afternoon. People crowded the wharf near the steamboat, pressed forward to see him, and repeatedly cheered "the defender of the people's rights and the supporter of the Constitution and laws of the country."[21]

Although mixed, the results of the New York City election

generally satisfied the Whigs. Tammany's mayoral candidate, Cornelius Lawrence, squeaked through by 181 votes out of 35,000 cast. But the Whigs captured a seventeen to fifteen majority on the city council, thus gaining control of a million dollars a year in patronage. "The Common Council is reformed, and we shall succeed in the great fall election," exulted Hone. "It is a signal triumph of good principles over violence, illegal voting, party discipline, and the influence of office-holders." To celebrate their victory, the Whigs held a great *fete* at Castle Garden on April 15. Three pipes of wine and forty barrels of beer were set out to refresh parched Whig throats. When the meeting broke up, six or eight thousand men formed a procession, and marched off the Battery, preceded by a band. Having learned that Webster (who had declined an invitation to attend the celebration) was visiting his sister in Greenwich Street, a "large number" formed before the house in a solid body and called for him. Wrote Hone:

> He made his appearance at one of the windows and was received with shouts that rent the air. I was admitted through the basement, and having passed through the kitchen, came into the front room as Mr. Webster began to address the multitude. His address was full of fire, and was received with rapturous shouts. After he retired, he was called again, and spoke a few words more, when the mighty mass moved off as they came, with order and propriety.[22]

From New York, Webster went to Washington. At Baltimore, ten thousand people with flags flying lined the shores as his boat approached the wharf, and he mounted to the upper deck and addressed the crowd. Horace Binney, who was traveling with him, was called upon to speak, but slipped away to the Exchange, where he sat for a moment with Representative Edward Everett of Massachusetts, who was on his way to Philadelphia. Binney then started back to Barnum's, but as he approached the hotel, to his astonishment, "Mr. Webster was at it again, and the street covered with a dense mass of thousands." When he concluded, Binney was called for, and being recognized, had no alternative but to say a dozen words or so. "The excitement, *hurras,* etc., etc., were extraordinary, and evidence of extreme irritation," he wrote later.

"I ask absolution of my good bishops for this Sunday's miscon-
duct. Think of it, and think of what public life might make of
me. . . . I am ashamed, and I am glad of it."[23]

Webster's friends were already laying the groundwork for a
formal nomination at a later date. Rufus Choate, who was promoting the Senator's candidacy from Washington, said it was of
"great consequence" that his name "should be prominently held
forth—public attention drawn to him—his claims & efforts more
particularly & anxiously dwelt upon—with a view to ultimate
. . . action."[24]

The starting point for Webster's candidacy was Massachusetts.
He must have his own state behind him before waging a campaign for wider support. Whig strength centered in the densely
populated eastern counties of Suffolk (Boston), Essex, and Worcester; in the Connecticut Valley, Franklin and Hampshire were
rural Whig strongholds. The party drew its members from the
propertied classes and their economic dependents. Bankers,
merchants, ship-owners, and cotton manufacturers dominated
both the National Republican and Whig organizations. Wealthy
businessmen like Abbott Lawrence, Nathan Appleton, and William Sullivan formed a small leadership clique which conferred
with such politicians as Webster, Governor Levi Lincoln, and
John Davis of Worcester to select candidates for office and make
campaign plans. Small tradesmen, native laborers, who resented
the Jacksonian appeal to immigrant labor, and other urban elements followed the lead of wealthier neighbors. In country districts and small towns, the well-to-do farming class, especially
those engaged in sheep raising who wanted tariff protection and
those who sold agricultural products to urban markets, were
Whigs.[25]

This conservative hegemony was now challenged by a rising
Jackson party of country folk, the small farmers of the western
and southern counties; the fishermen of Gloucester, Marblehead,
and Cape Cod; and the poorer classes in general who wanted a
change in the established social order. "Between 1824 and 1848
Jacksonian Democracy [in Massachusetts] was essentially a rural
party in rebellion against the dominance of urban wealth and

social position."[26] Joining this protest against the conservative *status quo* was a tiny Workingmen's Party, "preponderantly a rural and agrarian party, with an urban complement of carpenters, masons, and ship-caulkers," and the Antimasons, recruited from the rural areas of the west and south—as much from the humble country folk in the National Republican party, who had been accustomed to vote for conservative candidates—as from the Democrats.[27] The Masons among the leadership of Massachusetts Whiggery were unwilling to abandon their order; and, consequently, the Antimasons of the Bay State, contrary to their tendency in other states, were threatening to align themselves with the Democrats. David Henshaw, the leader of the Jackson party machine in Boston, and his Masonic friends were beginning to lose control of the Democratic organization to leaders of the rival "country" faction. This accelerated the Antimasonic movement toward Democratic affiliation. United, the minority parties would be almost as numerous as the dominant Whig organization and might drive it from power. Such a defeat would prostrate Webster's candidacy for President, and eliminate him from serious contention.

Antimasonic support was also essential to Webster hopes in other key northern states, particularly Pennsylvania and New York; and it was imperative that his friends conciliate the Massachusetts Antimasons, lest their opposition injure his prospects nationally. "We rejoice here to see the efforts toward composing the anti-masonic question," Rufus Choate wrote from Washington—"God grant we may reunite our friends in Mass—& elsewhere for the great struggle with the Regency which is coming."[28]

Conciliation, however, proved no easy matter. In the fall of 1833, John Quincy Adams accepted the Antimasonic nomination for governor chiefly in the hope of receiving the National Republican one as well. Edward Everett and other National Republican leaders promised as much. But "a Masonic faction in Boston," which sent thirty-five of the sixty-three town delegates to the National Republican convention at Worcester, blocked Adams' nomination; and the meeting chose instead John Davis. Even the sacred name of Webster failed to sway the delegates to

Adams' cause. As a further gesture of hostility to Antimasonry, the platform declared: "To us it seems that the fears of the Anti-masons are altogether exaggerated and extravagant, and that their objects, so far as they are pursued by political measures, are utterly unworth the countenance of an intelligent people."[29]

In the fall election no gubernatorial candidate received a majority. Davis won the largest vote, but Adams came second and made large gains for the Antimasons in eastern Massachusetts, chiefly at the expense of the National Republicans. The Democratic candidate, Judge Marcus Morton of the State Supreme Court, a leader of the "country" faction, was third in the balloting. The Workingmen's candidate, Samuel C. Allen of Northfield in the Connecticut Valley, received 3,459 votes, 727 of them in the western county of Hampshire, where the movement was strongest. Adams refused to allow his name to go before the legislature, and the Senate elected Davis over Morton.[30]

Adams had dinner with Webster in Washington on January 7, 1834, and told him it was his purpose, if possible, to bring back to the National Republican party in Massachusetts its Antimasonic portion; that the tendency of the party was to go over to Jacksonism; that they had been encouraged to this by the Antimasonic opinions and, perhaps, pledges of Morton and his friends, and that they were prejudiced against Davis on the ground that he was entirely under the influence of Masonry; but that they might be induced to support his administration if it should disentangle itself from the Masonic faction. According to Adams, Webster concurred in all these opinions and said that all the other members of the Massachusetts delegation, except Baylies and Osgood, concurred with them as well. Bates, Choate, Grennell, and Silsbee were Masons, and were all willing to abandon the institution. "Mr. Webster told me his own impression upon Masonry—which had always been unfavorable; said his father had always disliked the institution, and had brought him up in the dislike of it."[31]

Webster assured Adams that all the Masons in the delegation would join in recommending the total abandonment of Masonry, and that he saw no reason to object to any act making all extrajudicial oaths, "whether of Anti-Masonry or about the sea-serpent," penal. He thought, too, that by electing one or two distinguished Antimasons as members of the Governor's Council a conciliatory disposition might be manifested, and he named a Mr. Fuller and a Mr. Bailey. Adams agreed that would be a measure "both just and conciliatory."[32]

But despite these assurances, the National Republicans in Massachusetts continued hostile to Antimasonry. Only eighteen of the forty contests for the state senate had been decided by the necessary majority vote. According to state law, vacancies were to be filled by the House, and here the National Republicans had a majority. The Antimasons, as the second party in size, had expected a share of the Senate seats, but instead the National Republicans filled all twenty-two vacancies with their own men, in entire disregard of who had received pluralities in the election. This action proved to Adams' satisfaction that the National Republicans were as "exclusive and intolerant as ever."[33]

The National Republicans also coldly received Antimasonic legislation. They did kill a bill to facilitate the building of the Masonic Grand Lodge in Boston, and approved a legislative committee to investigate and report on Masonic activities; but there the concessions stopped. The Senate refused to compel Masons to testify before the committee and replaced its strong recommendation against extrajudicial oaths with a much milder measure.

Not surprisingly the Antimasonic legislators, at once up in arms, moved toward the Democratic party. The National Republicans could not get the necessary Antimasonic votes to pass resolutions condemning Jackson's removal of the deposits. Caleb Cushing, a National Republican member of the House from Newburyport, and a Mason, complained to Webster that their party was "paralyzed" by the Antimasons, who were working in perfect harmony of action with the Jacksonians. Cushing wanted Adams to use his influence to placate the Antimasons and heal the breach.[34] Webster sent Edward Everett to see Adams with Cushing's letter; but the old man, feeling that he had done everything possible to unite the two parties, refused any further aid.

Mr. Cushing must look to himself and his party for the failure
of all my endeavors to conciliate. I had given fair notice and
warning both to Governor Davis and Mr. Webster, from both of
whom I had received encouraging assurances of conciliation to
the Anti-Masons, instead of which every possible thing had been
done to fret and exasperate them: all their candidates for the
Senate had been swept off the board; not one Anti-Mason had
been elected to the Council; a fraudulent law against unlawful
oaths was now in concoction to baffle and deceive them; and just
now the Senate had refused to grant to the joint investigating
committee the power to send for persons and papers; and now
their aid was implored to pass National Republican resolutions
in favor of the bank. It was impossible for me to do anything
more with them, and I did believe they would go over to Jacksonism. I had done all I could to prevent it, but in vain.[35]

At length, the National Republicans grudgingly undertook
some further measures of conciliation. The Masonic Grand Lodge
of Massachusetts agreed to surrender its charter to the state. The
legislature passed a bill punishing the giving of extrajudicial oaths
by fines of from $200 to $500. In March 1834, a caucus of the
National Republican members of the legislature adopted a resolution inviting the Antimasons to forget all differences of opinion
upon "minor subjects," and to join with them in opposition to
Jackson. But the Antimasons replied that they could not "hon-
estly listen to any pretended 'measure of conciliation' with any
party, which has not for its basis, the extirpation of Free Masonry
from the land."[36] Edward Everett, who was sympathetic to the
tenets of Antimasonry, warned Cushing that the tendency to an
Antimasonic-Jackson party coalition was "now strong"; and that
if the Masons did not allow their order to go down, "utterly, openly, & without qualification," Massachusetts would give her vote
to Morton for Governor and Van Buren for President. He and
Cushing considered it expedient that Webster's name should not
be publicly connected with the Antimasonic controversy; and the
Senator stayed quietly in the background, while they urged the
abolition of Masonry.[37]

During the summer of 1834, Cushing and Rufus Choate, who
had resigned his seat in Congress at the end of the session in June,
rode through eastern Massachusetts persuading Masonic lodges to

give up their charters voluntarily. In August, Masons from Worcester County met together and resolved that "the Masonic Institution has . . . become unnecessary . . . [and] should now be voluntarily dissolved by its members." Masons in Essex, Hampshire, Franklin, and Hampden counties adopted similar resolutions. In reporting the Worcester resolves, *Niles' Weekly Register* predicted they would have a "powerful effect in the eastern states, for the recommendations will be generally adopted."[38] Charles Francis Adams noted in his diary on September 4 that "Governor Davis and a considerable number of Masons in various parts of the State are lending their aid to dissolve the Institution."[39]

Webster was optimistic about the chances of a political union with the Antimasons in the fall election. "As to the Anti Masons, I confess I do not see how they can now, with any justice, set up a candidate in opposition to you," he wrote Governor Davis, who was a candidate for a second term.

> What could any Govr. do, more than you have done? You have supported a law for the abolition of secret oaths; & all such oaths are abolished. You have now recommended to Masons, to surrender their Charters; many of them, I trust, will follow your advice. It seems to me that reasonable and just men must see that your course has been candid, just, & conciliatory; & that there is no fair ground to oppose your re-election. . . . Some effort, some action, some setting of an example, is all that is wanting, on either side, as it appears to me, in order to bring the great body of Whigs and Anti-masons, in this state, into harmonious action.[40]

Under the circumstances, the Antimasonic leaders seemed to have doubted the wisdom of nominating a distinct Antimasonic candidate for governor. They asked Adams' opinion, and he advised them to support Davis. They decided, however, under the spur of the radicals, to put forth their own ticket, and in a large state convention, chose Adams' friend, John Bailey of Dorchester, for their gubernatorial candidate, and Heman Lincoln of Boston, for the lieutenant governorship. The Antimasons were still angry at the rejection of Adams by the National Republicans the previous year and that party's coldness earlier in 1834. Anti-

masons scoffed at the charge that Adams had been rejected because he had deserted the Federalist party years before, and cited
the Masonic denunciation of Edward Everett, on whom, they said,
both parties would have been willing to unite. Benjamin Hallett,
radical editor of the Antimasonic Boston *Daily Advocate,* talked
of a union with Morton and the Democrats and declared that
*"Conciliation* as used by the supporters of Mr. Davis means
nothing but *submission."*[41]

The Massachusetts Whigs carried on an active and enthusiastic campaign in the state election that produced an overwhelming
victory. The total vote for governor increased 24.3 per cent over
1833; and Davis' total (44,802) was 78.1 per cent higher than the
National Republican vote the year before. He had 54.7 per cent
of the total vote, a sharp increase over his position in 1833, while
the Democratic candidate, Marcus Morton, showed no change at
all, with 19,255 votes (24.8). Bailey, the Antimasonic candidate,
received 10,975 votes, but this was 40.9 per cent less than Adams
won in 1833. Allen, again the choice of the Workingmen, polled
only 2,602 votes, which was 24.9 per cent less than his total the
previous year. The bulk of the Workingmen's vote was cast in the
rural counties of Hampshire, Franklin, Bristol, and Middlesex.
Allen's following had begun to return to the Democratic party.[42]

The great increase in the Whig vote may be attributed to
dissatisfaction with the fiscal policies of the Jackson administration. The Whigs also increased their majorities in the state
legislature and elected ten (eventually eleven) of the twelve
congressmen from the state. One Whig paper, the Newburyport
*Herald,* crowded: "MASSACHUSETTS ERECT!—The success of the
Whig party in this state is beyond all expectation. A week
since, we trembled lest the Jackson men should carry the legislature, and baffle the choice of a Whig U. S. Senator. Now it is
certain that the majority in both Houses will be overwhelming."
In honor "of the glorious triumph of good principles in this
Commonwealth," about five hundred persons, including Webster,
Everett, Governor Davis, and Abbott Lawrence, attended a Whig
festival at Charleston on November 21, secure in the knowledge

that for the moment, at least, their hegemony was unchallenge-able.[43]

The losers could only console themselves with a long view. George Bancroft told Everett it would be some years before a "popular party" could become powerful in Massachusetts. But he predicted, "it will rise, and within six years it will culminate. Webster will run for the presidency, and will get at most 24 votes. Van Buren will come in; and Massachusetts will come over to his support."[44] To Van Buren, Bancroft wrote that there was some chance of "an interesting electioneering campaign" in the state in 1835. The Whigs had won in 1834 under false pretenses; "and though the personal popularity of Mr. Webster is such, that he himself can readily secure a great majority of the votes, yet his popularity is not transferable. *The whig leaders cannot dispose of the state.* The democratic party is steadily gaining ground among the yeomanry."[45]

Meanwhile, Webster's friends continued to promote his candidacy for the presidency. Cushing and Choate, with Webster's approval, began negotiations to secure control of the influential Boston *Atlas,* which they proposed to turn into an active Webster journal. The *Atlas,* which published its first issue on July 2, 1832, had thundered a resounding *no!* to the proposed National Republican-Antimasonic coalition behind Adams in 1833 and had urged the Worcester convention to settle its nomination on John Davis. It argued that the acceptance of Adams would place the affairs of the state under the management of the Antimasonic leaders. Richard Hildreth, who was active in the Boston councils of the National Republicans and sometimes served as secretary for party meetings, owned a small share in the paper and claimed to have originated this policy of no union with Antimasonry. The *Atlas'* conduct prompted Webster to observe that if the Whig party desired to maintain its respectability, such papers as the *Atlas* must cease to be its organ.[46] However, by gaining control of the *Atlas,* the Webster Whigs could eliminate one vocal obstacle to a union with the Antimasonic party.

John O. Sargent, a talented editorial writer on the *Atlas* staff, was partially responsible for the interest of the Websterites

in the paper. "He is young, but manly . . . [and] intelligent,"
Cushing informed Webster after an interview with Sargent. "He
enters, heart & soul, into all our hopes & wishes." Cushing added
that he had pledged Webster's Boston friends to two things: "1.
Indemnity;—2. Any requisite intellectual aid, without limitation
of quantity. . . ."[47] These terms were satisfactory to Sargent and
Richard Haughton, general editor and majority owner, arrangements were quickly completed, and Sargent became associate editor. Hildreth, whose health was weakening under the strain of
his political and journalistic activities, sold his share in the paper
to Haughton and left Boston for Florida. He complained that
Haughton was determined to back Webster as the Whig presidential candidate, a policy with which he disagreed.[48]

Circular letters were mailed to all sections of the country on
behalf of Webster's candidacy. One letter, in the handwriting of
Edward Everett and also signed by Warren Dutton, Abbott Law-
rance, Franklin Dexter, and Rufus Choate, was sent on August
20 to John Woods, editor of the Hamilton (Ohio) *Intelligencer*.
After expressing the need to concentrate the opposition to the
administration in support of the strongest candidate for the
presidency, the letter said in part:

> It appears to us . . . clear to demonstration, that no person can
> be brought forward, with the slightest hope of success, who does
> not unite the strength of the National republicans and Anti-
> masonic parties.—Nothing short of this will carry either of the
> great middle states (including Ohio); and it is doubtful whether
> any thing short of it will carry New England.—We are confident
> that Mr. Webster alone can unite those two parties in New
> England and New York;—and that he is as likely as any other
> individual to do it, in Pennsylvania and Ohio.—His prospect
> therefore, at present, is far better than that of any other individual
> named as a Whig candidate.

The letter requested information as to the views of Ohioans on
Webster's candidacy, and asked, "should your general opinion
coincide with ours," for Woods' opinion as to the time and
manner of a formal nomination.[49]

Some of the Webster Whigs were eager to enter the contest

without further delay. John O. Sargent warned Cushing that "every day that now is lost in getting into the field is a loss to the Cause—and a serious loss. We have too much work before us."[50] From Mobile, Alabama, Edward Gazzam urged Webster to make an immediate journey to the South. "*This* is the moment for action, this is the fairest starting point," he declared. "A visit from you at the present juncture would stir public opinion & give it the much needed impetus." The *"constitutional* Whig" who won the South or any considerable part of it would in all probability be the next president, since northern and western Whigs would eagerly support such a candidate. Such an opportunity, Gazzam warned, might "never again occur in favor of a northern statesman."[51] Webster, however, did not visit the South, correctly believing that he could not rally any major support in that area.

In August 1834, Associate Justice Joseph Story of the United States Supreme Court contributed his mite to the Webster cause by publishing anonymously in *The New England Magazine* an essay entitled "Statesmen—Their Rareness and Importance. Daniel Webster," in which he gave a sketch of the Senator's political career "as an incitement and admonition to the young and ambitious, and a consolation and hope to the old and the contemplative." By indirection, the Judge set forth his friend's qualifications as a statesman for the presidency:

> . . . by statesmen I mean men, who have profoundly studied the nature, science and operations of governments in general; men, who intimately understand our relations with foreign states and foreign policy; men, who have taken a large survey of all our national interests, agricultural, manufacturing, commercial, political; men, who have not only acquired some knowledge of the theory of statistics and political economy, but who have had a thorough experience in public business and public measures; men, in short, who may safely be entrusted with public affairs, because they have high talents and solid requirements, and unite with these a liberal spirit, a thorough acquaintance with the details, as well as with the principles of government, and a lofty ambition, as well as an honest purpose, to serve their country, and to give permanence to its institutions and interests. Such men, and no other men, are entitled to the character of statesmen.

He had been led to these remarks, Story concluded, not so much by any general views of the subject, as "by the immediate contemplation of the character and services of a great statesman now living. I mean DANIEL WEBSTER."[52]

A Whig victory in the November election in New York was to signal Webster's formal nomination. Young William H. Seward of Auburn was the Whig candidate for governor against the incumbent, William L. Marcy, and the contest was considered a trial of Whig strength in the coming presidential election. According to Philip Hone, "the great election in the State of New York is to decide whether the principles of General Jackson are approved and ratified by the people, and whether Mr. Van Buren is to be his successor: for these important questions are left to the decision of this State, and the test will be the result of the election."[53] The Whigs, amidst great enthusiasm, proclaimed themselves the true successors of the "Whigs of 1776," and Webster added to their zeal by avowing himself in a letter to be "the son of a father who acted an humble part in establishing the independence of the country," and saying, "I have been educated from my cradle in the principles of the Whigs of '76!"[54]

Van Buren wrote to Jackson from Saratoga Springs on August 7 that "our success is as certain as any future event, that is dependent upon the vote of the people, can possibly be." He reported that Webster was to meet a "congregation" of Whigs at Saratoga on August 13, "but if they give him any assurances of anticipated success, he would, if he had the sense and observation in such matters of which he is destitute, detect the falsity of their representation, in the woe-begone countenances which they carry about."[55] Nor was Van Buren mistaken in his prophecy of victory. The Whigs were soundly trounced by the Democrats, who returned Marcy to office by a large majority, and elected Democratic senators in seven of the eight senatorial districts.[56]

Webster was in New York City during the election as a member of a special Senate committee on banking and on the evening of November 4 made a "short and eloquent speech" to a large Whig gathering from the steps of his hotel, Washington Hall.[57] John Tyler, who was visiting the North at this time, wrote his friend William Gordon that he was half pleased that the Democrats had won in New York; for his visit to the Northeast had fully satisfied him that, "if New York declared against Van Buren, Webster would at once . . . [have been] proclaimed a candidate for the Presidency." The South, unable to accept him, would have either been forced into the arms of some other northern or western man, or the contest would have given rise to a feeling of hostility between the sections. "This election avoids these contingencies," exulted Tyler. "Webster is driven from the field, and the whole North is in a state of despair."[58]

Webster, contrary to John Tyler's hopes, was not "driven from the field" by the Whig defeat in the New York election, but the emergence of rival "pretenders" in the fall of 1834 made his own formal nomination more imperative than at any earlier time. The Washington *National Intelligencer,* the chief organ of the Whig party, declared on September 17, 1834, that it was too early to select a man to oppose Van Buren; but friends of each candidate were afraid that others would benefit from their own delay.[59] In the North, in addition to Webster, Clay, and McLean, Louis McLane of Delaware was mentioned as one who could rally disaffected Jackson men against Van Buren; and supporters recommended that he be "brought out" by a nomination in a western state.[60]

In the South, state rights men weighed the claims of Calhoun, ex-Governor George Troup of Georgia, and Benjamin Watkins Leigh and Littleton W. Tazewell of Virginia; but the opposition candidate who finally emerged in that area was Senator Hugh Lawson White of Tennessee. Originally a warm supporter of the President, White "soured" on the Kitchen Cabinet and also quarreled with Jackson over the appointment of Senator John M. Clayton to a special committee on the tariff during the nullification crisis.[61] State pride, hostility to Martin Van Buren, and a sincere desire to see White elected President, led some of his friends in Tennessee to urge the old man's nomination. White discouraged these efforts until Jackson, in August 1834, vowed to make his name "odious" in Tennessee if he accepted a nomination. White now became more receptive to friendly persuasions and accepted a nomination made by a majority of the Tennessee delegation in Congress (December 23, 1834). The White camp maintained throughout the 1836 campaign that his candidacy did not involve any personal hostility to the President, and they denied any connection with national parties. But their action in bringing White forward against the expressed wishes of Jackson made inevitable their ultimate absorption into the Whig party.[62]

State Rights Whigs found the Tennesseean an acceptable lesser evil. "Between Van Buren and White our party cannot long hesitate," wrote John Tyler. "White has been against the old Democracy for two years only, and on two or three important subjects; Van Buren always,—for upon no one point of policy have we agreed with him. Judge White would give a pure administration; Van Buren would seek to fortify himself by all the means in his power. For one, I do not hesitate a moment in my choice."[63]

The Whigs viewed this split in the Jackson party in Tennessee with keen delight, since they expected the White candidacy to weaken Van Buren not only in the South but in the North as well. Thomas Hart Benton wrote later that the anti-Jackson men had secured White's assent to a nomination by playing upon the vanity of his second wife, a divorcee who "having made an immense stride from the head of a boarding-house table to the head of a senator's table, could see no reason why she should not take one step more, and that comparatively short, and arrive at the head of the presidential table." As soon as White was committed to the race, a Whig congressman from Kentucky wrote a friend in his district: "*Judge White is on the track, running gayly, and won't come off; and if he would, his wife won't let him.*"[64] Van Buren charged in his autobiography that while he himself had no special claims on the Judge, it had cost White "a great effort" to separate from Jackson, who had admonished him and his wife "in his usual unreserved and emphatic way, of the consequences of the step he was about to take." But, "Mr. [John] Bell of Tennessee . . . and Mr. Webster, by his attentions particularly to a member of the Judge's family as well as to him, overcame his scruples."[65]

Van Buren's accusation does not prove Webster's part in persuading White to accept a nomination; but he certainly looked upon the Tennesseean's candidacy as helpful to his own. And perhaps he used personal charms on White and his wife. In a letter to Jeremiah Mason some months later, Webster predicted that "Mr. White's nomination is likely to be persisted in. Neither you nor I have ever believed it would be easy to get Southern votes for any Northern man, and I think . . . Van Buren will lose the whole South. This schism is calculated to give much additional strength to our party."[66]

Still, there was a danger that White's candidacy might gain some currency in the North to the detriment of Webster's prospects. The Boston *Atlas* therefore argued that Jacksonian antecedents precluded White's support by any genuine Whig. To sustain such a man would make the Whig creed "a Lie, and the history of the Whigs a tissue of infamy." There was no common ground on which the northern Whigs could meet the friends of Judge White. "Jacksonism runs in every drop of his blood; it was born in his flesh, and has been bred in his bone." What policy then should the Whigs pursue? The *Atlas* had a ready answer: "Let us sustain one of our own men, a believer in our own creed, a champion of our own principles, a minister of our own faith." The Whigs should stand firm and take advantage of the schism in the enemy's ranks. Van Buren's game was up in the South; White would rout him in every southern state. Why then should the Whigs talk of abandoning the Whig candidate, whosoever he might be, when there was every prospect of his receiving more electoral votes than either of the administration candidates, White and Van Buren, thus increasing the chances of his election?[67]

Although the *Atlas* had not mentioned Webster by name, he was clearly the "minister of our faith" that the paper had in mind. The prospect of White's candidacy convinced the editors of the *Atlas* that Webster's nomination should not be delayed further; and on December 17, 1834, the paper formally raised his flag. Webster, said the *Atlas,* would unite the full strength of the

friends of the Constitution; and it urged his supporters throughout the country to present his claims to the people.[68]

The Massachusetts legislature was about to meet and a
nomination by the Whigs of that body would be an excellent
beginning for Webster's campaign. His friends, however, were
divided over such an endorsement. "I should not be surprised
to hear that Webster was nominated by the Legislature of Mass.,"
Congressman Millard Fillmore of Buffalo wrote to Thurlow Weed
from Washington. "Some of his friends here are in favor of it—
some opposed to it."[69] The Boston *Atlas* rebuked those of Webster's friends who thought a nomination now premature: "The
Time Has Come. If we mean that Mr. Webster should be a
candidate—because we believe him the man most worthy of the
office—we have not a day or an hour to lose. In political movements, delay is defeat,—doubt is death."[70]

Webster wanted an immediate nomination. To Jeremiah
Mason, he wrote from Washington on January 1, 1835, that it
must be made now if ever. He thought McLean was already nominated in Ohio and many Whigs were supporting him because
they had no other choice. If a resolution to make a nomination
in Massachusetts should be adopted, not only should it be done
at once, but in the meantime, "notice of the intention should be
given to friends in the neighboring States, and especially in New
York, that they may prepare for it." "Let us know *here* the moment anything is determined on," Webster urged. "Be sure to
*burn* this letter and assure yourself that I write such letters to
nobody else."[71]

Mason replied that a nomination would be made in a few
days, barring some unforeseen obstacle. He had seen Governor
Davis, whose feelings and opinions were, as always, "entirely
right." Some others, who were rightly inclined, but habitually
slow in action, wanted to have a more formal communication with
the Massachusetts delegation at Washington on the subject, and
letters had been sent, but Mason thought the representatives
would not wait for replies. One objection to the nomination was
that it would cause Webster to resign from the Senate at the end
of the session. This was stated vaguely, on the authority of a

supposed intimation from the Senator himself. However, some of Webster's friends had denied this, and Mason thought a resignation for this cause alone would be considered false delicacy. At all events, it seemed to Mason there was no necessity to decide then. "If the election is to be finally determined in the House of Representatives, the presence of a candidate at Washington, without exerting any improper influence, will be advantageous."[72]

Caleb Cushing was working diligently in Boston to gratify Webster's desire for a nomination. On January 3, he wrote to the Senator that if the Massachusetts legislature would cordially make a nomination, there was "a great *net balance* of argument in favor of it being done." At the same time, Cushing admitted that a postponement might be necessary to make the nomination certain and to have it done "handsomely and *con amore.*" He was working through the *Atlas,* the *Courier,* and the *Centinel* to gain popular support for the move.[73] However, even before the nomination was definitely assured, the Webster Whigs in Washington found it necessary, because of McLean's nomination in Ohio, to signify to political leaders in different parts of the nation that a nomination of Webster could be expected in Massachusetts.[74] Although Cushing once more assured Webster that a nomination would be made "cordially and spiritedly," the delay continued.[75] H. W. Kinsman, a member of the legislature from Newburyport, explained to Webster that among the "honest, sincere" Massachusetts Whigs there were three parties: "Those who are more friendly to Mr. Clay as a candidate than to yourself; Those who prefer you, & wish to make a nomination forthwith and, those, who, although you would be their first preference, yet wish to wait to take up the strongest whig candidate who may appear in the field. . . ." The cause of delay, however, lay with a group of *"waiters upon Providence,"* pseudo-Whigs who were secretly opposed to Webster's candidacy. These men, among whom Edward Everett's brother Alexander was the most prominent, were warning that his prospects were hopeless and that the Whigs should take up some more popular candidate. In spite of these croakers, a preliminary meeting of the Whig members of the legislature on

January 16 had agreed to hold a formal nomination meeting later in the week.[76]

This opposition to Webster's candidacy in his own state indicated the chief obstacle to the success of his campaign for the Whig nomination—the belief among many party leaders that he could not beat the cool-blooded Van Buren. "I may say that I have not conversed with any member from any quarter of the Union who say that he thought either Clay or Webster stood any chance of success," Millard Fillmore advised Thurlow Weed; he viewed Webster's nomination as "the most extreme folly."[77] Senator Willie P. Mangum was convinced that no opposition man could be elected President. "They may mar, but they can't make," he predicted flatly. "This opinion prevails here almost universally.—Clay is off—Calhoun is off—& Webster, tho anxious for a nomination, must soon find that overwhelming defeat is inevitable." Mangum thought the Whigs would probably be reduced to a "choice of evils"—McLean, Van Buren, or White.[78]

Predictions of certain defeat did not dishearten loyal Websterites. The Webster press in Boston now called for a nomination. "It is time that Mr. Webster should be fairly brought before the Country," declared the *Atlas,* and whence could his nomination come with greater propriety than from his own constituents, his own friends, the legislature of his adopted state? The Whigs throughout the country were impatient for a nomination. "They must have a candidate in the field, and speedily. There is no time to be lost." The Boston *Daily Advertiser and Patriot,* noting McLean's nomination in Ohio, warned that if the Whig members of the legislature were to present a candidate to the people, "the sooner it is done the better." The Boston *Courier* also urged prompt action by the legislature.[79]

In Washington, Webster and his friends were being bombarded with anxious inquiries about the Boston proceedings. "Letters recd. today from Columbus and Cincinnati ask urgently what is doing, or to be done, in Massachusetts," Webster informed Mason, adding that "there has been some impatience here, in regard to the proceedings in Boston. . . ."[80] Edward Everett wrote to Cushing: "I am glad the nomination is likely to move *bon train.* A member of Congress from Maryland has just expressed a strong wish for the prompt action of Massachusetts. What else is to check the progress of Judge M'Lean [sic] in Ohio or elsewhere?—"[81]

These last promptings were unnecessary. On the evening of January 21, 1835, 315 Whig members of the Massachusetts legislature met in Representative Hall, Boston, and unanimously nominated Webster to his fellow citizens as a candidate for the presidency, "not as a citizen of Massachusetts, . . . [but] as a citizen of the United States, as the 'man of the country' thoroughly acquainted with all its interests, . . . and [as] a most firm, zealous and eloquent defender of the glorious constitution under which we live."[82]

Webster told Jeremiah Mason that Washington friends found no fault with the manner of the nomination; measures were underway to produce similar action in New York, Vermont, and other states. "If Massachusetts stands steady, and our friends act with prudence, the union of the whole Whig and anti-masonic strength is certain," Webster predicted. "Everything indicates that result. Judge McLean already talks of retiring. His nomination seems coldly received everywhere. Unless Indiana should come out for him, I see no probability of any other movement in his favor." As for White, his candidacy seemed certain to weaken Van Buren in the South and, indirectly, in the North as well. "If Mr. W. [White] appears likely to take the South, it will be seen that Mr. Van Buren cannot be chosen by the people; and as it will be understood that Mr. White's supporters are quite as likely to come to us, in the end, as to go to Van Buren, his cause will lose the powerful support which it derives from an assured hope of success."[83]

Webster expected White would weaken Van Buren in the North enough to give Webster victory there. If no candidate had a majority and the election went into the House of Representatives, the White men would support him rather than Van Buren. "Mr. Webster's friends," explained the *United States Telegraph*, "hope that the south will separate from Mr. Van Buren, and so far weaken him in the north, that he [Webster] can become his successful competitor in that quarter! and, by uniting the north, and northwestern states, secure his election."[84]

The Boston *Atlas* reported a most gratifying response to Webster's candidacy. ". . . not a mail arrives that is not filled with the approbation of every quarter of the Union," it boasted. "Never were the prospects of the Whigs more cheering,—we had almost said certain. . . . DANIEL WEBSTER is no longer the candidate of the Whigs of Massachusetts, for the patriots of the Union have adopted him." The *Atlas'* Washington correspondent thought Webster's prospects were daily brightening. Men, who a few weeks earlier had deprecated his nomination as premature and impolitic, now altered their tone, and admitted that he stood as good a chance as any candidate in the field. The *Atlas* declared that the leading newspapers in New York City were favorable to Webster's candidacy, as were the Whig journals in Maine. In Ohio, it noted that the Columbus *State Journal,* the Dayton *Journal,* the Massillon *Whig,* the Cleveland *Western Reserve Chronicle,* the Senaca *Whig,* and the Steubenville *Herald* were "friendly to Mr. Webster." Also cheering was the willingness of the *National Intelligencer* to sustain his nomination if it gained general support among the "friends of the Constitution."[85]

Webster was fortunate in having several bright young men working in his behalf, whose political prosperity depended on his own. In addition to Choate, Cushing, and Edward Everett, Robert C. Winthrop actively supported his nomination with effective speeches during the campaign of 1836. He also wrote a number of circulars and resolutions, including, at the request of Hiram Ketchum, the greater part of an *Address to the People of the United States* for a public meeting in New York City. The talented Winthrop, twenty-six in 1835, had read law in Webster's office for almost three years before his admission to the Boston bar in 1831. A member of the Whig State Central Committee, he was also on the staff of Governor John Davis.[86]

Webster was in a position to reward loyal service with high public office. He was presently urging the claims of Edward Everett as the Whig candidate for governor in 1835, to succeed John Davis. Despite the efforts of Everett, Choate, and Cushing to

unite the state's Whigs and Antimasons by advocating the abolition of Masonry, the parties had not settled their differences.
Everett was sympathetic to Antimasonic tenets, and that party
might endorse his nomination. Such a result, Webster believed,
would hasten the merger of the two parties in Massachusetts and
strengthen his own candidacy among Antimasons elsewhere. As
he explained to Jeremiah Mason: "It has been thought that his
nomination would bring back a portion of the Anti-Masons to a
union with the Whigs. . . . We need our whole strength in Massachusetts, and a cordial cooperation of the Anti-Masons, in Massachusetts, *in other things* [i.e. Webster's candidacy], would have
greatly beneficial effects in N. Y. and Pa. . . . If practical, a
pacification of the Anti-Masonic question is doubtless highly
desirable."[87]

To make room for Everett, Governor John Davis was to go to
the United States Senate in place of Nathaniel Silsbee, who refused to be a candidate for re-election. It was up to the two houses
of the Massachusetts legislature, voting separately, to agree upon a
replacement. The House of Representatives selected Davis, but
the Senate chose John Quincy Adams. Then news arrived from
Washington that Adams was supporting Jackson's French spolia-
tion claims policy. "On one thing our Legislature may depend,"
reported the Capital correspondent of the Boston *Atlas*. "*J. Q.
Adams is considered here too uncertain for the Senate.* Our
friends do not esteem him *safe*. His recent movement on the
French Question has alarmed and confused them." It was also
rumored that Adams had not yet given up all hope of being again
nominated for the presidency. "Be assured that the true friends
of Mr. Webster can pursue but one course in this matter; if they
wish to subserve his cause, . . . they will send John Davis to the
Senate."[88] The Senate promptly switched to Davis, who was there-
by elected. According to Charles Francis Adams, his father had
been sacrificed to advance the selfish ambitions of Webster, Davis,
and Everett.

> Mr. Webster and Mr. Everett have been flattering each other.
> The latter not suffering from any feeling of friendship to prevent
> his sacrificing my father has been instrumental in pursuing this

empty sound, this Legislative nomination of Mr. Webster to the
Presidency, in exchange for which Mr. Webster urges the trans-
lation of Davis to the Senate so that room may be made for Mr.
Everett next year.  Mr. Webster knows very perfectly what he
is about in all this.  The presence of my father in the Senate
would hardly be agreeable to him.[89]

Young Adams was very bitter against the Webster Whigs for
their arrogant treatment of his father, but comforted himself with
the thought that the senior Adams "may do the country better
service in the House," and that "Perhaps Mr. Webster may feel
the consequences of his low intrigue even yet."  To embarrass the
Whigs, Adams recommended to Benjamin Hallett, editor of the
leading Antimasonic journal in the state, the Boston *Daily Advocate,* that the Antimasons take the initiative and nominate
Everett for governor first, so that the Whigs "must now take the
candidate of the Antimasons or they must risk a separation and
a total defeat."[90]  This was done.  On February 26, an Antimasonic
general meeting in the State House at Boston unanimously nominated Everett.  On the morning of February 27, the *Atlas* favored
endorsing the Antimasonic nomination.  That evening, one
hundred and sixty-six Whig members of the legislature met in
caucus, and of these, all but nine voted for Everett.  According to
Charles Francis Adams, the nomination had been dictated mainly
by the seventy Boston members.  The country and Masonic Whigs
had preferred Isaac Bates.  "I do not know whether the result will
be affected but one thing is certain," Adams noted with satisfaction in his diary, "that the party is shaken at this moment by
the dissatisfaction of the whole western section of the State.  So
far, so good."[91]

An adjustment had also been made by which the Lieutenant-
Governor, Samuel F. Armstrong, was to perform the duties of
the Executive for the remainder of Davis' term.  But he, too, did
not enjoy being casually thrust aside in favor of Everett.  John
Quincy Adams confided this fact to his diary on June 15, 1835:

Mr. Armstrong is much dissatisfied with the arrangements of the
triumvirate, Webster, Edward Everett, and John Davis, in
disposing of the Government of the Commonwealth as they

did to Edward Everett. He thinks the people of the Common-wealth will not ratify the bargain. But the people of the Commonwealth have been so managed for the last six years that I know not how long they will be kept in leading-strings.[92]

The ex-President was right; the people did ratify the arrangement. In the election on November 9, 1835, Everett carried Boston by nearly two to one over his Democratic opponent, Marcus Morton; and his majority in the state was 12,328 votes; yet the total vote was small and fell below that of the previous year. Everett had 7,200 fewer votes than Davis in 1834, while Morton gained 5,900. Samuel Armstrong, running as an independent, polled 1,901 votes. The Democrats had not only gained the support of the Workingmen, but had won a large number of Antimasons, and recovered much of the ground they had lost the year before.[93]

Meanwhile, Webster pressed ahead with his candidacy. His friends urged an electioneering tour of the West, to extend at least as far as Kentucky and Indiana, and Webster was "fully persuaded it would be a highly useful thing." Although the tour did not materialize, after Congress adjourned he accepted an invitation to visit Pennsylvania. With his wife and daughter, he traveled to Harrisburg, the state capital. The state legislature was in session, and he took the opportunity to quietly seek support for his candidacy among its members. A committee representing both houses tendered him a public dinner, which he declined because of lack of time. After visiting briefly in Lancaster and York, Webster went on to New York City. Friends there found him in good spirits after the warm reception in Pennsylvania. He dined with Philip Hone who noted in his diary that "the great senator has been more uniformly cheerful during his present visit than I have ever seen him, and he is, when 'in the vein,' one of the best talkers in the world."[94]

Webster deftly shook off the incubus of the Bank of the United States. In some remarks in the Senate on February 26, on a bill to regulate the deposits of the public money, he announced that he considered the question of renewing the Bank's charter as entirely settled:

It cannot be renewed. Public opinion, very unfortunately, as I
think, for the country, has decided against it; and while there is
a strong and prevailing sentiment in the minds of the community
against a measure, it is quite useless to propose it. For myself,
I shall take no part in any attempt to renew the charter of the
bank. The people have decided against its continuance, and it
must expire.

Nor would he join in any attempt thereafter to establish a new
national bank, until the consequences of its absence satisfied the
country of its utility or necessity.[95]

   This declaration brought a sharp letter from Nicholas Biddle.
The president of the Bank objected to Webster's remarks because
he had stated as a fact, without qualification, that the people had
decided against the Bank, without implying any doubt of the
correctness of that opinion other than to call it unfortunate.
Such a sentence "seemed to imply an indifference—a coldness—
an alienation from the Bank—and a desire to disconnect yourself
with it." Such impressions were unjust both to Webster and to
his friends in the Bank; and Biddle thought the best mode of
rectifying them would be to revise the speech. "You can do this
with more freedom because Mr. Jaudon tells me that when the
speech appeared while he was in Washington, he mentioned to
you that it was not what you said. Remember then what you did
say and I think you will fall into this train of thought." Biddle
suggested some "hints," complimentary of the Bank, and its directors and officers, which would remove a little soreness where
none ought to exist. He concluded: "Make something like this
in your short—sententious—lapidary way and I will accept it as
the epitaph of the Bank."[96] Webster ignored Biddle's suggestion.

   In April 1835, the Webster campaign suffered its first serious
setback since his nomination three months earlier. In the spring
contests in Connecticut and Rhode Island, the Democrats elected
their gubernatorial candidates by small majorities. The Jackson
party in Connecticut had majorities of 11 in the Senate (16-5)
and 46 in the House (126-80). In Rhode Island, the Whigs retained control of the legislature by the slim margin of 3 seats in
the Senate and 2 in the House and reelected former Governor

Knight to the United States Senate.[97] These Whig defeats reflected upon Webster as New England's favorite son. John Quincy Adams noted with satisfaction that the elections represented "another downfall of federalism under the name of Whigs." "The nomination of Daniel Webster as a candidate for the Presidency by the Whigs of the Massachusetts legislature," he pontificated, "has settled the State of Connecticut for Van Buren, and Massachusetts will stand alone in her glory."[98]

These defeats made Webster Whigs redouble their efforts. In April, Perkins, Marvin, and Company published a two volume edition of Webster's speeches. A second edition of Knapp's life of Webster was printed and distributed. To counter charges that Webster was disloyal during the War of 1812, Caleb Cushing prepared for the newspapers an account of Webster's patriotic conduct in 1814, when a British attack on Portsmouth, New Hampshire, was expected. Webster himself attended the 60th anniversary celebration of the battle of Lexington, where he delivered the sentiment: *"Lexington common—In '75 a field of blood—in all coming time a field of glory."* In distant Louisiana, ex-senator George A. Waggaman endorsed Webster for the presidency, and in a letter to members of the Louisiana legislature, recommended that they nominate him as the Whig candidate.[99]

Boston Whiggery also rallied to its "Godlike" candidate. An address signed by approximately 350 of the town's leading citizens called on "The Whigs of Boston and its vicinity and others friendly to the nomination of Daniel Webster for President of the United States" to assemble at historic Faneuil Hall on the evening of May 28, 1835. The meeting organized with John C. Gray as president and adopted fifteen resolutions offered by Charles P. Curtis approving Webster's nomination by the Whig members of the legislature and setting forth the grounds on which his candidacy would be supported. The meeting called upon:

> our friends—the friends of liberty, by whatever name they are designated, throughout the union, on all who reverence the constitution, on all who wish for a government of laws and a charter of civil rights, to descend to their children, to rise as

one man, and go with us; to forget local preferences and individual partialities; to act on pure principle; to hasten to the rescue of the country, and to assign the highest trust, in the disposal of the people, to the man of whom it was declared by William Lowndes, that 'the north had not his equal, nor the south his superior.'[100]

At this time a widespread and vigorous White press in the North was causing some concern among the Webster Whigs. Even in New England, a number of newspapers had raised the White flag, including the Bridgeport (Conn.) *Republican,* the Pawtucket (R.I.) *Chronicle,* and the Boston *Age.* On May 4, 1835, S. S. Southworth, who John Quincy Adams called a political writer for hire, wrote to Senator Mangum that "I proceed to Boston to-morrow, to take charge of a newspaper to be devoted to the political interests of Judge White." The Webster journals met this challenge by reiterating White's Jacksonian antecedents. The Boston *Courier* carried this argument one step further; not only was White objectionable to all good Whigs on the same grounds as Van Buren; but, in addition, he was "a nullifier, and an ultra 'State Rights' advocate."[101]

Fiery Duff Green, editor of the Washington *United States Telegraph,* a Calhoun organ, was a vigorous supporter of White's candidacy. On April 11, Green issued the prospectus for a campaign edition of the *Telegraph* to be published weekly for twelve months beginning June 1, 1835. "The Extra Telegraph," he announced, "will sustain the election of Hugh L. White, as the candidate whom the people have designated as the opponent of Martin Van Buren." Since Webster seemed the chief obstacle to White's candidacy in the North, Green launched a vigorous campaign to drive him from the field by charging that Webster and Van Buren were playing the same political game; both were laboring to build up a northern confederacy; both relied on northern votes. Van Buren, however, had played this game with more skill, and Webster could not count upon the support of a single northern state. Unless he had the energy and virtue to withdraw, he would be compelled to play the "puppet in Mr. Van Buren's hands, as a scarecrow to frighten the South into Mr. Van

Buren's support, or else sink down into the acknowledged partisan of his hated rival."[102]

Webster's ever faithful Boston *Courier* met Green's assault with a counterblast. It warned that by attacking Webster the *Telegraph* was fighting in Van Buren's cause, for White could not get an electoral vote north of the Potomac River. Those who were opposed to the administration must either go for Webster or go to sleep. With its present views of White's disposition and character, vowed the *Courier,* "we would as soon cut off the hand that writes this sentence and throw it to the first hungry dog that passes, as use it to support his pretensions to the Presidency."[103]

The *Telegraph's* savage attacks caused Webster to have second thoughts about the effect of White's candidacy. He now feared that the whole Whig strength in the country "was either to be frittered away, or melt into the support of Mr. V. Buren." In this pass he turned to Nicholas Biddle. "I do not know whether anything can be done to change the course of things; but I am fully persuaded, that if anything *can* be done, it is to be done in Penna.," he wrote on May 9, 1835.

> Your people are awake to political subjects, in consequence of the pendency of an election for Govr. If those who are likely to unite in support of Mr. Ritner could unite also in making some demonstration on National Subjects [i.e. Webster], & do it immediately, it might possible have some effect. . . . Our Friends here receive letters, every day, & from Pa. as well as from other quarters, calling on them to do more, & say more. But they hardly see what more *they* can do, or say. The sentiment of Massachusetts is known; & it would seem to be for the consideration of others, whether it should be seconded.[104]

Webster also complained to Biddle about the reluctance of the *National Intelligencer* to support a candidate for the presidency: "If Messrs G & S. [Gales and Seaton] are not disposed to support, at present, any named candidate, they might, at least, preach the necessity of supporting *a* Whig candidate—*some* Whig Candidate. We are in danger of breaking up & dividing." If Biddle deemed this suggestion worthy of attention, Webster asked him to give some "availing hints, in the right quarter."[105]

In their quest for support, the Websterites now turned their attention to Ohio, where the state legislature was to assemble on June 18. The Pittsburgh *Advocate,* a leading Antimasonic journal in western Pennsylvania, urged the Whig majority in that body to nominate Webster for President and General William Henry Harrison of Ohio for Vice-President. With Massachusetts and Ohio united behind his candidacy, the *Advocate* predicted that "Webster and the constitution" would secure the support of three or four additional New England states, as many western states, and Maryland, Delaware, and probably Pennsylvania, among the middle states.[106] With this editorial in mind, Edward Everett asked Biddle if he thought such a nomination "would have a very decisive effect," to exert his influence in Ohio to bring it about. He proposed that Biddle drop a line to some influential persons, members of the legislature, or others, at Columbus. "There is really strength enough in the Country, to elect Mr. W. [Webster], if it could be concentrated & cordially united, in his support," he pleaded. Biddle in reply assured him that "as far as regards any movement in Ohio, the proper suggestions thro' the proper channels have already been made from this quarter." While this was hardly specific enough to be very encouraging, Everett declared that he was "right glad you have put things in train beyond the mountains."[107]

In fact no nomination came from Ohio, but in Rhode Island a Whig state convention assembled at Newport on June 24 and recommended Webster to the people as a man who enjoyed "the unqualified confidence" of the friends of the Constitution and the Union. The Richmond *Whig* predicted this nomination would be seconded by the Whigs of Pennsylvania, Maryland, and New York. Even more gratifying to the Webster Whigs was the endorsement of the *National Intelligencer.* On July 11, 1835, in an editorial entitled "The Prospect Before Us" the paper, after a canvass of possible Whig candidates, announced its support of Webster and eulogized him as "no time-serving truckling politician," but "ever the champion of Liberty and the Laws." At the same time, the *Intelligencer* recognized that many southern Whigs would not vote for Webster because of his nationalist views, and cordially recommended Hugh Lawson White as a suitable southern candidate. It stressed the importance, by whatever means necessary, of defeating Van Buren.[108]

This endorsement seemed to put a final stamp of approval on Webster as the candidate of the anti-Jackson men in the northern states. White's campaign there, in spite of Duff Green's best efforts, had not caught fire. The single exception was Illinois where the Whigs endorsed a ticket of five White electors, all of whom were anti-Van Buren and Jackson men.[109] As Webster had predicted, McLean's campaign had not prospered outside of Ohio; and he was about to withdraw from the canvass. Clay, unable to secure support from Whig leaders, gave up the struggle reluctantly. On July 14, 1835, he wrote John Bailache, Whig editor of the *Ohio State Journal,* that the action of the Whig members of the Ohio legislature in approving of McLean had been "highly injurious" to his (Clay's) prospects. He elaborated, "Ohio had been considered as a State which (Jackson out of the way) would certainly bestow her suffrage on me, if I were a candidate. It was believed, and probably is yet believed, that no candidate would unite so much strength in opposition to Mr. Van Buren as I could." He did not see the wisdom of selecting as a candidate, "an original friend of Jackson, in preference to all who had been uniform in opposition to him," a policy which looked too much to support expected from the Jackson ranks, while underestimating the loss from Whig aversion, or apathy and indifference. Clay recalled his statement that he would only be a candidate if there were strong reasons to believe that he would not again be defeated, and such a situation did not now exist.[110]

The only other announced northern Whig candidate, besides Webster, was General William Henry Harrison who had been nominated by public meetings in Pennsylvania and the Northwest. But as late as July 11, 1835, the *National Intelligencer* dismissed his candidacy as unlikely to gain any considerable support among northern Whigs. In September, a prominent Jackson leader in Ohio predicted that Harrison would "have his run of six months and then run down like an old wooden clock."[111]

Whig journals were soon busily promoting their own favorites

for the vice-presidential nomination on a Webster ticket; among
the most frequently mentioned were Harrison, Joseph Vance, and
Thomas Ewing, all of Ohio.[112] A paper in that state, noting that
the "apprehension of defeat from the votes of the illiterate and
prejudiced multitude" had alone restrained the Whig party from
proclaiming Webster as its candidate, declared that "fears of this
kind have now in great measure been removed." Webster was
decidedly more popular in the northern states than Van Buren;
and if the election were thrown into the House of Representatives,
there could be little doubt of his success.[113]

## NOTES

1. Charles Francis Adams Diary, September 20, 1833, Adams Papers, Massachusetts Historical Society, Boston.

2. Adams, *Memoirs*, IX, 35.

3. C [sic], "Whig and Tory," *New-England Magazine*, VII (1834), 234-238.

4. Carroll, *Whig Party*, pp. 118-126; Dixon Ryan Fox, "The Economic Status of
the New York Whigs," *Political Science Quarterly*, XXXIII (1918), 501-518; Clement
Eaton, *Henry Clay and the Art of American Politics* (Boston, 1957), pp. 113-114;
Edward Pessen, "Did Labor Support Jackson?: The Boston Story," *Political Science
Quarterly*, LXIV (1949), 262-274.

5. Charles Grier Sellers, Jr., "Who Were the Southern Whigs?" *American
Historical Review*, LIX (1954), 335-346.

6. Adams, *Memoirs*, IX, 105-106, 108.

7. Gerald M. Capers, *John C. Calhoun-Opportunist: A Reappraisal* (Gainesville,
1960), pp. 178-179; Calhoun to Francis W. Pickens, January 4, 1834, in J. Franklin
Jameson (ed.), "Correspondence of John C. Calhoun" *Annual Report of the
American Historical Association*, II (1900), 328. (Hereafter cited as "Calhoun
Correspondence.")

8. Andrew Lane to John McLean, January 31, 1835, quoted in Francis P. Weisenburger, *The Passing of the Frontier, 1825-1850* (vol. III of *The History of the
State of Ohio*, ed. Carl Wittke [Columbus, 1941]), p. 294.

9. Quoted in Morison, *Life of Otis*, II, 299.

10. Robert C. Winthrop, Jr., *A Memoir of Robert C. Winthrop* (Boston, 1897),
p. 17. (Hereafter cited as Winthrop, *Memoir*.)

11. Hammond to Thomas Ewing, March 27, 1834, quoted in Francis P. Weisenburger, *The Life of John McLean: A Politician on the United States Supreme
Court* (Columbus, 1937), p. 97.

12. Adams, *Memoirs*, VIII, 505, 537.

13. Washington *National Intelligencer*, October 30, 1833; *Niles' Weekly Register*,

XLVI (1834), 153, quoting Hamilton (Ohio) *Intelligencer*, March 26, 1834. McLean's candidacy can be followed in the two books by Weisenburger already cited.

*14.* Follett to Henry Clay, January 10, 1833, in L. Belle Hamlin (ed.), "Selections from the Follett Papers, I," *Quarterly Publication of the Historical and Philosophical Society of Ohio*, V (1910), 75.

*15.* Van Deusen, *Henry Clay*, p. 298; Willie P. Mangum to Duncan Cameron, February 7, 1834, *Mangum Papers*, II, 74-75; Webster to Jeremiah Mason, February 1, 1835, *Writings and Speeches*, XVI, 251.

*16.* Calhoun to Lewis S. Coryell, August 10, 1834, "Calhoun Correspondence," 340.

*17.* Adams, *Memoirs*, IX, 188.

*18.* Ostrom to Daniel Webster, January 21, 1834, Webster Papers.

*19.* Bayard Tuckerman (ed.), *The Diary of Philip Hone, 1828-1851* (New York, 1889), I, 95. (Hereafter cited as Tuckerman, *Hone Diary*.)

*20.* *Ibid.*, p. 98; Clay to Peter B. Porter, April 11, 1834, quoted in Reed, "Emergence of the Whig Party in the North," p. 133.

*21.* Tuckerman, *Hone Diary*, I, 99.

*22.* *Ibid.*, pp. 101-102.

*23.* Binney to "H", April 21, 1834, quoted in Charles C. Binney, *The Life of Horace Binney* (Philadelphia, 1903), pp. 120-121.

*24.* Choate to Warwick Palfray, Jr., January 31, 1834, "Choate Letters," 87.

*25.* This analysis of Massachusetts Whiggery is taken from Darling, *Political Changes in Massachusetts*, pp. 182-183; Arthur B. Darling, "Jacksonian Democracy in Massachusetts, 1824-1848," *American Historical Review*, XXIX (1924), 274-276; and Kinley J. Brauer, *Cotton versus Conscience: Massachusetts Whig Politics and Southwestern Expansion, 1843-1848* (Lexington, 1967), pp. 15-16.

*26.* Darling, "Jacksonian Democracy," 272, 275-277.

*27.* Arthur B. Darling, "The Workingmen's Party in Massachusetts, 1833-1834," *American Historical Review*, XXIX (1923), 81-86; George Hubbard Blakeslee, "The History of the Antimasonic Party" (Unpublished doctoral dissertation, Harvard University, 1903), II, 291-293.

*28.* Choate to Warwick Palfray, Jr., January 31, 1834, "Choate Letters," 87.

*29.* Blakeslee, "Antimasonic Party," II, 294-300; Adams, *Memoirs*, IX, 16, 20.

*30.* Darling, *Political Changes in Massachusetts*, pp. 115-116.

*31.* Adams, *Memoirs*, IX, 71.

*32.* *Ibid.*

*33.* John Quincy Adams to Charles Francis Adams, January 31, 1834, quoted in Martin B. Duberman, *Charles Francis Adams, 1807-1886* (Boston, 1961), p. 50.

*34.* Cushing to Daniel Webster, February 23, 1834, Caleb Cushing Papers, Manuscript Division, Library of Congress. (Hereafter cited as Cushing Papers.)

*35.* Adams, *Memoirs*, IX, 103-104.

*36.* Blakeslee, "Antimasonic Party," II, 307-310.

37. Everett to Caleb Cushing, March 2, 1834, quoted in Claude M. Fuess, *The Life of Caleb Cushing* (New York, 1923), I, 140; Everett to Caleb Cushing, March 12, 23, 1834, Cushing Papers.

38. Blakeslee, "Antimasonic Party," II, 311-312; Fuess, *Caleb Cushing*, I, 142; *Niles' Weekly Register*, XLVI (1834), 447-448.

39. Charles Francis Adams Diary, September 4, 1834.

40. Webster to John Davis, August 14, 1834, *Writings and Speeches*, XVI, 242-243.

41. Blakeslee, "Antimasonic Party," II, 315; Darling, *Political Changes in Massachusetts*, p. 123.

42. Darling, *Political Changes in Massachusetts*, p. 127; Blakeslee, "Antimasonic Party," II, 316; Reed, "Emergence of the Whig Party in the North," pp. 193-195.

43. Quoted in Reed, "Emergence of the Whig Party in the North," pp. 195-196; Boston *Daily Atlas*, November 24, 1834.

44. George Bancroft to Edward Everett, November 17, 1834, quoted in Mark Antony DeWolfe Howe, *Life and Letters of George Bancroft* (New York, 1908), I, 214.

45. George Bancroft to Martin Van Buren, January 8, 1835, Van Buren Papers.

46. Donald E. Emerson, *Richard Hildreth. Johns Hopkins University Studies in Historical and Political Science*, Ser. LXIV, no. 2 (Baltimore, 1946), pp. 49-50; Richard Hildreth, *My Connection with the Atlas Newspaper* (Boston, 1839), pp. 4-7.

47. Fuess, *Caleb Cushing*, I, 146; Cushing to Daniel Webster, August 9, 1834, Cushing Papers.

48. Caleb Cushing to John O. Sargent, August 13, 1834, Cushing to Daniel Webster, n.d., Cushing to Daniel Webster, August 10, 1834, Cushing Papers; Fuess, *Caleb Cushing*, I, 148; Emerson, *Richard Hildreth*, p. 51.

49. John Perry Pritchett (ed.), " 'Friends' of the Constitution, 1836," *New England Quarterly*, IX (1936), 679-683.

50. Sargent to Caleb Cushing, September 1, 1834, Cushing Papers.

51. Gazzam to Daniel Webster, September 20, 1834, Webster Papers.

52. Story is identified as the author in William W. Story (ed.), *Life and Letters of Joseph Story* (Boston, 1851), II, 171.

53. Tuckerman, *Hone Diary*, I, 116-117.

54. Frederick W. Seward (ed.), *William H. Seward: An Autobiography from 1801 to 1834. With a Memoir of His Life, and Selections from His Letters, 1831-1846* (New York, 1891), p. 237. (Hereafter cited as Seward, *Autobiography*.)

55. Van Buren to Andrew Jackson, August 7, 1834, *Jackson Correspondence*, V, 279-280.

56. Glyndon G. Van Deusen, *Thurlow Weed: Wizard of the Lobby* (Boston, 1947), p. 89.

57. Tuckerman, *Hone Diary*, I, 117.

58. Tyler to William Fitzhugh Gordon, November 9, 1834, quoted in Armistead C. Gordon, *William Fitzhugh Gordon, A Virginian of the Old School: His Life,*

*Times and Contemporaries, 1787-1858* (New York, 1909), p. 293. On July 21, 1835, the Albany *Argus*, in commenting upon the expense accounts submitted by the Senate Finance Committee, noted: "To Mr. Webster, $202.40 *mileage from Boston to New York and back*. And when was this journey performed? We answer, at the period of the New York election, when and where Mr. Webster addressed the populace, and when and where it was understood, had the election resulted differently, Mr. Webster was to have been nominated for the Presidency by acclamation." See also Tuckerman, *Hone Diary*, I, 118.

*59.* Washington *National Intelligencer*, September 17, 1834; *ibid.*, quoting Raleigh *Register*, n.d.

*60.* John Spear Smith to Thomas Finley, September 3, 1834, in Isaac Joslin Cox (ed.), "Selections from the Torrence Papers, I," *Quarterly Publication of the Historical and Philosophical Society of Ohio*, I (1906), 92-95.

*61.* Willie P. Mangum to William A. Graham, December 28, 1834, *Mangum Papers*, II, 261; John Tyler to William Fitzhugh Gordon, quoted in Gordon, *William Fitzhugh Gordon*, p. 294; Lunia Paul Gresham, "The Public Career of Hugh Lawson White," *Tennessee Historical Quarterly*, III (1944), 309.

*62.* See Powell Moore, "The Revolt Against Jackson in Tennessee, 1835-1836," *Journal of Southern History*, II (1936), 335-359.

*63.* Tyler to Colonel Thomas Smith, May 8, 1835, quoted in Tyler, *Life and Letters of the Tylers*, I, 517. See also [Benjamin Watkins Leigh] to Willie P. Mangum, April 14, 1835, *Mangum Papers*, II, 331.

*64.* Benton, *Thirty Years' View*, II, 185.

*65.* Fitzpatrick, "Autobiography," p. 226n.

*66.* Webster to Jeremiah Mason, February 6, 1835, *Writings and Speeches*, XVI, 253.

*67.* Boston *Daily Atlas*, December 12, 15, 20, 1834.

*68. Ibid.*, December 17, 1834.

*69.* Fillmore to Thurlow Weed, December 28, 1834, in Frank H. Severance (ed.), *Millard Fillmore Papers. Publications of the Buffalo Historical Society*, vol. XI (Buffalo, 1907), pp. 156-157. (Hereafter cited as *Fillmore Papers*.)

*70.* Boston *Daily Atlas*, December 22, 1834.

*71.* Webster to Jeremiah Mason, January 1, 1835, *Writings and Speeches*, XVI, 245-246.

*72.* Mason to Daniel Webster, January 8, 1835, quoted in G. J. Clark (ed.), *Memoir, Autobiography and Correspondence of Jeremiah Mason* (Kansas City, Missouri, 1926), p. 345.

*73.* Cushing to Daniel Webster, January 3, 1835, quoted in Fuess, *Caleb Cushing*, I, 168.

*74.* Webster to Jeremiah Mason, January 10, 1835, *Writings and Speeches*, XVI, 247. In late December 1834 a caucus of "Democratic-Republican" members of the Ohio legislature met and recommended McLean as a candidate for the presidency. *Niles' Weekly Register*, XLVII (1835), 313. Everett told Cushing that "We have written to our friends in Ohio not to be perturbed at Judge M L's nomination: —Munroe of the Balt. Pat. says it produces no effect" (Everett to Caleb Cushing, January 9, 1835, Cushing Papers).

75. Cushing to Daniel Webster, January 10, 1835, quoted in Fuess, *Caleb Cushing*, I, 169-170.

76. Kinsman to Daniel Webster, January 18, 1835, *Letters of Webster*, pp. 191-193.

77. Fillmore to Thurlow Weed, December 28, 1834, *Fillmore Papers*, XI, 156-157.

78. Mangum to William A. Graham, December 17, 1834, *Mangum Papers*, II, 247.

79. Boston *Daily Atlas*, January 6, 1835; Boston *Courier*, January 12, 1835; Boston *Daily Advertiser and Patriot*, January 12, 1835.

80. Webster to Jeremiah Mason, January 22, 1835, *Writings and Speeches*, XVI, 248-249.

81. Everett to Caleb Cushing, January 22, 1835, Cushing Papers.

82. Boston *Daily Atlas*, January 22, 1835; see also *Niles' Weekly Register*, XLVII (1835), 379. Charles Francis Adams commented on the nomination as follows: "The Legislature last evening actually nominated him as a candidate for the Presidency. The game is up for Massachusetts" (Diary, January 22, 1835).

83. Webster to Jeremiah Mason, February 1, 1835, *Writings and Speeches*, XVI, 249-251.

84. Washington *United States Telegraph*, March 14, 1835.

85. Boston *Daily Atlas*, February 5, 9, 28, 1835; Washington *National Intelligencer*, March 12, 1835.

86. Winthrop, *Memoir*, pp. 13-14.

87. Webster to Jeremiah Mason, January 10, 1835, *Writings and Speeches*, XVI, 247-248.

88. Boston *Daily Atlas*, February 13, 1835.

89. Charles Francis Adams Diary, February 5, 1835.

90. *Ibid.*, February 7, 17, 1835; Charles Francis Adams to John Quincy Adams, February 27, 1835, Charles Francis Adams Letter Book, 157, Adams Papers.

91. Charles Francis Adams Diary, February 28, 1835.

92. Adams, *Memoirs*, IX, 242-243.

93. Darling, *Political Changes in Massachusetts*, p. 191; Frothingham, *Edward Everett*, p. 129.

94. Webster to Jeremiah Mason, February 6, 1835, *Writings and Speeches*, XVI, 253; *Niles' Weekly Register*, XLVIII (1835), 62, quoting Harrisburg *Telegraph*, n.d.; William Frederic Worner, "Daniel Webster in Lancaster; Observance of His Death," *Lancaster County Historical Society Papers*, XXVIII (1924), 118-120; Washington *National Intelligencer*, March 25, 1835, quoting New York *Commercial Advertiser*, n.d.; Tuckerman, *Hone Diary*, I, 136.

95. *Writings and Speeches*, VII, 200-201.

96. Biddle to Daniel Webster, April 6, 1835, President's Letter Book No. 5. B.U.S. In 1836 Biddle secured a charter from Pennsylvania, which enabled the Bank to continue in operation until 1841, when, because of the economic depression and costly speculations, it was forced to close its doors.

97. *Niles' Weekly Register*, XLVIII (1835), 130, 186, 202.

*98.* Adams, *Memoirs,* IX, 233-234. However, a Providence (R.I.) Whig had another explanation. He declared that the party had been defeated because many Whigs "stopped by the roadside to quarrel about masonry, anti-masonry, anti-slavery, anti-brandy, gin and cold water, orthodoxy, heterodoxy, Fanny Wright, Beelzebub, and rail roads. *Thus we quarreled, split and divided—the well organized forces of the administration marched up in the mean time and carried all before them"* (Boston *Courier,* April 18, 1835).

*99.* Fuess, *Daniel Webster,* II, 43; *Niles' Weekly Register,* XLVIII (1835), 75, 152.

*100.* Boston *Courier,* May 26, 30, 1835; *Niles' Weekly Register,* XLVIII (1835), 243-244.

*101.* Boston *Daily Atlas,* December 12, 15, 20, 1834; Boston *Courier,* March 3, April 13, 1835; S. S. Southworth to Willie P. Mangum, May 4, 1835, *Mangum Papers,* II, 342; Adams, *Memoirs,* IX, 311.

*102.* Washington *United States Telegraph,* April 11, 18, 20, 1835.

*103.* Boston *Courier,* April 13, 14, May 14, 1835.

*104.* Webster to Nicholas Biddle, May 9, 1835, *Biddle Correspondence,* pp. 250-251. The Whigs of Pennsylvania were supporting Joseph Ritner, the Antimasonic candidate for governor.

*105.* Webster to Nicholas Biddle, May 12, 1835, *ibid.,* pp. 251-252.

*106.* *New-York American,* June 2, 1835, quoting Pittsburgh *Advocate,* n.d.

*107.* Everett to Nicholas Biddle, June 3, 1835, *Biddle Correspondence,* p. 253; Biddle to Edward Everett, June 10, 1835, President's Letter Book No. 5. B.U.S.; Everett to Nicholas Biddle, June 13, 1835, Biddle Papers.

*108.* *Niles' Weekly Register,* XLVIII (1835), 315, quoting Providence *Journal,* n.d.; Washington *National Intelligencer,* July 8, 1835, quoting Richmond *Whig,* July 3, 1835; Washington *National Intelligencer,* July 11, 1835.

*109.* Charles Manfred Thompson, *The Illinois Whigs Before 1846. University of Illinois Studies in the Social Sciences.* Vol. IV, no. 1 (Urbana, 1915), p. 53.

*110.* Clay to [John Bailhache], July 14, 1835, in Calvin Colton (ed.), *The Works of Henry Clay,* Federal Edition (New York, 1904), V, 394-395. (Hereafter cited as *Works of Clay.*)

*111.* Washington *National Intelligencer,* July 11, 1835; Thomas L. Hamer to James K. Polk, September 26, 1835, quoted in Weisenburger, *Passing of the Frontier,* p. 318.

*112.* Washington *National Intelligencer,* July 21, 1835, quoting Painesville (Ohio) *Telegraph,* July 10, 1834; *ibid.,* July 28, 1835; Albany *Argus,* July 28, 1835, quoting New York *Commercial Advertiser,* n.d.

*113.* Washington *National Intelligencer,* July 21, 1835, quoting Painesville (Ohio) *Telegraph,* July 10, 1835.

# THE STRUGGLE
# WITH OLD
# TIPPECANOE

6 The weakness of the Whigs lay in their disunity. They had trouble agreeing on how to select a candidate for 1836, let alone who the man should be. Some Whig leaders and papers recommended that the Whig congressmen make a caucus nomination, but this method of selection had been discredited in the election of 1824.[1] A national convention was also out of the question, since it would expose differences among the party's factions to public ridicule. "The truth is, that we Whigs of 1834 are a very impracticable set of fellows," William Seward confessed. "We are too independent to become good politicians. We all agreed that the Tories are ruining the country, and that it is our duty to avert the calamity. But each man must have his own way of averting it."[2]

The Whigs were therefore pleased when the Democratic convention at Baltimore in May 1835, with its carefully arranged nomination of Van Buren, furnished an excuse to avoid a national convention by damning it in turn as undemocratic and unrepublican. "The whole proceedings of the convention," said a

Baltimore newspaper, "has been management, management, management."[3] The office-holders who had taken part in "the Van Buren convention" were counted and their names published as proof that the national convention was actually a revival of "King Caucus" in an equally objectionable form. Tennessee sent no delegates to Baltimore; but determined that the President's home state should be represented, the convention seated Edward Rucker, a Tennessean who happened to be in the city, and permitted him to cast fifteen votes for Van Buren. The Whigs roared with laughter over the "Ruckerized" convention. In a more serious vein, the Illinois Senate adopted a resolution proclaiming that every person eligible to the office of President had an incontestable right to come forward as a candidate for it, without the intervention of caucuses or conventions. "We disapprove," said the Senate, "of the system of convention which Van Buren's party is endeavoring to thrust upon the American people, and we hold that this system is destructive of freedom of voting, contrary to republican institutions and dangerous to popular liberties."[4]

Whig strategists hoped to throw the election into the House of Representatives by running two presidential candidates, one each from the East-Northwest and South, who would represent, as Clay wrote, "the feelings and interests of each of the two great divisions of the party."[5] The *National Intelligencer* predicted that by such a course, the Whigs "*may* succeed in electing the candidate whom they particularly prefer; and they will certainly succeed in defeating the candidate [Van Buren] to whom they are *all* opposed." This would not rule out the possibility of uniting upon a single candidate after the election. State legislative caucuses or conventions, which would give "a more satisfactory expression of the public sentiment" than national assemblies, should select the nominees.[6]

Accordingly, friends of Hugh Lawson White entered his name in the race through legislative nominations in Alabama (January 1835) and Tennessee (October 1835). The Whigs gave him a clear track in the South. McLean's withdrawal in August 1835 left Webster, with nominations in Massachusetts and Rhode Island, an apparent clear field by default for the support of northern Whigs. In June the Washington *Globe* warned the Democratic faithful that Webster would be the Whig candidate in the North with the power of the Bank behind him. The fixed determination of the White and Webster men to adhere to their respective candidates, it charged, was with the common intention of making the election "ultimately the subject of regulation among the politicians in Congress." Reviving the corrupt bargain charge made effectively against Adams after 1824, the *Globe* predicted that under similar circumstances "Mr. Webster will bring into the House not only promises of political honors and Treasury emoluments—but the Ready Gold of the Bank, in glittering millions." The opposition would unite upon him to oppose Van Buren.[7]

Actually, northern Whig leaders were unenthusiastic about Webster's chance for success in the coming election and were quietly seeking a more popular candidate. The "Godlike's" aristocratic habits, Federalist taint, and legal-political association with the Bank of the United States, made him, in the political language of the day, an "unavailable" candidate in the opinion of Whig wire-pullers. In a survey of the presidential field in Ohio, editor John Bailhache said that while Webster's nomination was popular in New England, it did "not . . . stand the remotest chance of obtaining even a solitary vote in any of the Southern or Western States," and it "could not possibly succeed in Ohio." He emphasized that the nomination could not affect a "sufficient attendance at the polls to afford a reasonable hope of a favorable result."[8] The Clay men in the West were particularly hostile to him because of his flirtation with Jackson in 1833. Clay admitted that Webster's attainments were "greatly superior to those of any other nominated candidate," but acknowledged that "a general persuasion seems to exist that he stands no chance. I believe that, if he stood a fair chance elsewhere, by great effort, the vote of this State [Kentucky] might be given to him. In this opinion, however, I differ from many of my friends."[9]

In New York, William Seward revealed his awareness of Webster's liabilities when he told Thurlow Weed:

It is the height of madness to run Webster as a candidate. I believe nothing is left but that to exclude the Whigs from the sympathies of the People. The maniac who levelled his pistols at the president accomplished the most important part towards converting this Government into a monarchy. . . . The Whigs have hitherto stemmed this tide of popular delusion but let them identify themselves with the hereditary prejudice against Federalism and there will be no power left which can hold the delusion in check.[10]

A month later he added: "My conscience reproaches me for concurring with you in the disapprobation of Webster's nomination. I cannot support it, and why *because he is too great, too wise too pure.*—But I cannot doubt that it is our duty to endeavor to defeat Van Buren—To vote for Webster is indirectly to elect Van Buren—and to fix upon the Whigs the perpetual stigma of federalism."[11]

Jackson allegedly said Webster would never be President because he was "too far east, knows too much, and is too honest," and predicted the Whigs would choose a soldier in 1836. "They have had orators enough."[12] If the story was true, Old Hickory was a seer. The choice of those Whigs opposed to the New Englander's candidacy fell upon sixty-three year old General William Henry Harrison, once Governor of Indiana Territory and hero of the battles of Tippecanoe (1811) and of the Thames (1813) in the War of 1812. After the war, he served briefly and without distinction as a congressman and senator from Ohio. In 1828 he went to Colombia as American minister but proved an inept diplomat and was recalled by Jackson. Returning to his farm at North Bend, Ohio, he lived on the verge of poverty until friends obtained a position for him as clerk of the common pleas court in Cincinnati, so that he might pay debts and support his family. Still, "Old Tippecanoe" had much to recommend him as a candidate; a nationally known figure, he was uncommitted on controversial issues.[13]

The initial proposal of Harrison's name appeared in the *Pennsylvania Intelligencer* of December 14, 1834, possibly at the suggestion of some Ohioan,[14] and a public meeting in Dauphin County, Pennsylvania, formally nominated him on January 19,

1835. During the spring, his candidacy quietly gained strength, with a Cincinnati group who had formerly backed Clay active in starting the ball rolling.[15] By March, William H. Seward had decided that the old general offered the best hope of victory. "I have seen no suggestion which pleased me so much as that which presents General Harrison; certain it is, there is none so safe," he confided to a friend. "We can give him all the votes we can to anybody. If we fail with him, we are a patriotic party and a great one." In June, while traveling through Pennsylvania, Seward noted in his journal that "our friends at Harrisburg are earnest for the nomination of General Harrison for the presidency, and have done much to prepare the people's mind for that course."[16]

Harrison himself received the first suggestions that he run for the presidency with mixed feelings of wry self-deprecation and soldierly resolve. To General Soloman Van Rensselaer of New York, he wrote on January 15, 1835:

> I am the *Clerk of the Court of Common Pleas of Hamilton County* at your service. But I have news still more strange to tell you if you have not already heard it. Some folks are silly enough to have formed a plan to make a President of the United States out of this *Clerk* and Clodhopper! And amongst other reasons they assign is, that of my being the only one at all likely to overthrow the Champion of the Empire State. Now if he were only a Champion, however famed for deeds of noble daring in fair and open fields, an old Soldier could not well decline the contest. But then he is supposed to deal in an Art which forms no part of the tactics that you and I have learnt. But even with this advantage, I will not yield the field to him if I am selected for the combat, but will willingly give way to either of the more able and experienced Warriors that can be selected from the ranks in which I am enrolled.[17]

Because of his military record, Harrison had been brought forward for Vice-President by both the Webster and White forces.[18] But the General soon decided that the idea of being President was not so ridiculous after all, and when two Ohio editors placed his name with Webster's on a tentative Whig ticket, he authorized the Cincinnati *Whig* to state flatly that he would not accept the second spot on *any* ticket. In the late spring of 1835, he made a long-postponed visit to the Tippecanoe battle-ground, sailing up the Wabash and surveying the new towns of Terre Haute, Rockville, Crawfordsville, and Lafayette. A round of public dinners and festive balls introduced him to hundreds of people in that Indiana wilderness he had campaigned over twenty years before. He declined dinner invitations at Indianap-olis and Rushville, but was feted at Brookville in the southeastern part of the state. Harrison was well pleased with the reception. He spent the Fourth of July at Lawrenceburg, Indiana, and fol-lowing other social and military gatherings in his honor at Mad-ison and New Albany, Indiana, and Louisville, Kentucky, two prominent Kentucky papers, the Frankfort *Commonwealth* and the Lexington *Observer and Reporter* hoisted the Harrison flag, followed shortly by the Indianapolis *Journal* and the Richmond *Whig*.[19] With their own favorites out of the race, western sup-porters of Clay and McLean hastened to enroll in the Harrison ranks. "We have no hesitation in saying," declared the Louisville *Journal* in September, "that passing events strongly indicate to our minds, that General Harrison is to be the Whig candidate in the West."[20]

Nicholas Biddle laid down the campaign strategy for Har-rison in a now famous and often quoted letter to Herman Cope, president of the Cincinnati branch of the Bank and one of the General's managers. He wrote: "If Genl. Harrison is taken up as a candidate, it will be on account of the past, not the future. Let him then rely entirely on the past. Let him say not one single word about his principles, or his creed—let him say nothing—promise nothing. Let no Committee, no convention—no town meeting ever extract from him a single word, about what he thinks now, or what he will do hereafter. Let the use of pen and ink be wholly forbidden as if he were a mad poet in Bedlam."[21] Cope actually showed Harrison this remarkable and not very flattering letter, and after reading it carefully twice, the General said he was "more than all highly pleased" with this new evidence of Biddle's friendship for himself! "You have long been a favorite with him," Cope assured Biddle. "His prospects continue to brighten in the west; and from the number of letters he receives almost daily from highly influential Gentlemen in the east, north & south, I should judge him the most popular candidate of the opposition. His friends, here & elsewhere, have very generally given him the advice you suggest, and he appears disposed as far as possible to be governed by it. I hope on his own account he may."[22]

The Harrison journals now joined with the White press in deprecating Webster's prospects. Duff Green plunked a familiar chord. "Mr. Webster is now the most potent prop in Mr. Van Buren's scheme of power and ambition," he wrote, "because while Mr. Webster cannot compete with Mr. Van Buren in the North, he furnishes . . . the strongest, and the only apology which any Southern man can give for supporting Van Buren." Let Webster withdraw and the Whigs would have no difficulty in agreeing upon a candidate who would defeat "the scheme of unholy ambition." The pro-Harrison Cincinnati *Gazette* maintained that Webster's nomination had excited no enthusiasm while the General's had gone ahead of all others in public acceptance: "Harrison takes with the People,—why then, shall not the politicians adhere to him?"[23]

The Webster papers naturally decried the selection of a military candidate by the Whigs. The Pittsburgh *Advocate* warned that it would never support the nomination of "a second rate man" or "another 'military chieftain.'" Its candidate was Daniel Webster, "not *General* or *Colonel* Webster, but plain, unsophisticated, untitled, *Daniel Webster.*" The Boston *Atlas* said it would not oppose Harrison as long as his principles concurred with those the Whigs were struggling to maintain, but let him not be presented to Whig favor for his military achievements! "Let him not be put forward as the hero of Tippecanoe and the Thames. We have had enough of this species of military fustian and glorification." Still, the *Atlas* was forced to deny rumors that Webster was about to withdraw from the canvass. "His prospects are more encouraging than they were at the time of his original nomination," it insisted. "His cause has been daily gaining strength, silently and gradually it may be, but still at-

taining a growth the more healthy and vigorous on that account."
The *Atlas* urged the Whigs of Massachusetts to call meetings in
their principal towns to reaffirm their faith in Webster's candidacy.[24]

The Webster press also discounted Harrison's political following. The *New-York American* said his "real strength" was
nothing at present, "though by dint of 'drums, trumpets and
blunderbusses'—of hurras! for Tippecanoe and the Thames . . .
and such like expedients, his retainers may be swelled into an
imposing array. . . ." The Boston *Atlas* thought public feeling
in the West "very unsettled" in relation to Harrison. "We speak
advisedly when we say, that Mr. Webster divides the favor of the
people in that part of the country, [and] that in Pennsylvania his
name is still a tower of strength."[25]

In September, Webster visited Maine where the Whigs of
Cumberland and Penobscot counties had held conventions and
adopted resolutions in favor of his candidacy. He was honored
with public dinners at Bangor (September 25), where he dwelt
on the theme, "There is no usurpation so dangerous as that which
comes in the borrowed name of the people," and at Hallowell in
the Kennebec Valley (October 3); and he declined a Portland
dinner. His warm reception in Maine was widely publicized in
the Webster journals as a refutation of the charge made by the
Harrison and White press, that he did not "take with the people."[26]

Upon his return from Maine, Webster was presented with a
massive silver vase, commissioned by the citizens of Boston as a
testimonial of their gratitude for his congressional service as
Defender of the Constitution. More than four thousand people
packed the Odeon on the evening of October 12 to hear his acceptance address. Webster spoke upon his favorite theme—the Constitution—and warned his listeners that its character was being
altered by the diminution of the just powers of Congress on the
one hand, and in the vast increase of executive authority through
the use of the federal patronage on the other. Some check on the
President's removal power was necessary, and Webster affirmed
his own belief that a true interpretation of the Constitution would

place that power in the hands of the President *and* the Senate. "It is time to assert, on one hand, the just powers of Congress, in their full extent," he declared, "and to resist, on the other, the progress and rapid growth of executive authority."[27]

Webster's Odeon address contained no ideas he had not expressed on other occasions, but was widely reprinted in papers favorable to his candidacy as proof of his eminent worth and talents. Consistent with their conservative character, the Webster journals wished to maintain the standards for the presidency as they had existed before the rise of Jacksonian Democracy. The Whig candidate should have abilities and qualities of the highest order, and Webster was the only man in the field with these qualifications. "We go for Mr. Webster, because he is the fittest man," explained the *New-York American* loftily. "If the people are content to prefer inferior men, we must submit, but certainly are in no way called upon to contribute to such a result."[28]

The obvious disdain of the *American* for "the people" was characteristic of the well-to-do, conservative class which made up the bone and sinew of the Webster party. Rejecting the Jacksonian rhetoric and clinging to the aristocratic tradition of the Federalist and National Republican parties, this class was opposed to meeting Van Buren with a candidate possessing some of Jackson's popular qualities. Unfortunately for Webster, these were precisely the qualities which practical politicians like Thurlow Weed and William H. Seward recognized as essential for success in the coming election; and which they saw in Harrison. "The National Republican party has deceived itself by consulting and taking counsils [sic] almost exclusively from those in the highest walks of life," an Ohio congressman had lectured Webster in 1833. "The rank and file men however poll the votes."[29] And Webster, it was said, had little concern for the rank and file. Indeed the Democratic press imputed to him the sentiment, "Let Congress take care of the Rich, and the Rich will take care of the Poor." Webster disavowed the statement as "an entire and utter falsehood," but was on the defensive.[30] His distant kinsman, Noah Webster, wrote of his mortification "that men can be found in this country *weak* enough to suppose you or any respectable man capable of the meanness which could dictate such a declaration, or *wicked* enough to propogate it, knowing it to be false," yet admitted that "it is not improbable our country contains multitudes of persons who may fall under both descriptions."[31]

The taint of treason which the defunct Federalist party bore because of its role in the Hartford Convention also clung to Webster despite his repeated denials of any connection with that meeting. "He is considered as standing at the head of the old Federal party; and the sins of that party are visited on him," William Plumer had observed in 1833. "There is no great justice in this; but there are too many men in all parties who know how to use this circumstance to his prejudice."[32] Elisha Whittlesey warned Webster that there was a prejudice against New England in the southern and southwestern states to some extent: "Your locality will be against you—although the former division of parties does not exist in point of fact: you know how easy it is for a demagogue to blast the prospects of the finest man in the world, by crying out federalist."[33] Now in the heat of the canvass, as Plumer and Whittlesey had foreseen, old slanders were revived and sedulously circulated. Webster was once more forced to deny publicly any connection with the Hartford Convention. "If it would gratify yourself and friends," he assured one anxious inquirer, "I would give you sundry facts and dates, which show, what is strictly true, that I had no hand or part whatever in the Hartford Convention, and it is true that I expressed an opinion to Governor Gilman, that it would not be wise in him to appoint delegates. Further than this I have no recollection of interfering in the matter."[34] Still, it was true, as the Democratic press charged, that he had opposed the War of 1812, although the *National Intelligencer* said lamely that this opposition had been "atoned by a long period of devotion to the best interest of the country."[35]

The Webster Whigs were falling into confusion. Realizing this, the Harrison men pressed their advantage by carrying the General's campaign into the East. A Whig and Antimasonic meeting in Albany, New York, at which a thousand men were present, announced its support of Harrison's candidacy, along with that of the old Antimason, the popular New York congressman, Francis Granger, for Vice-President. Seward thought this action "precipitate and unwise" and pointed to the "hazard of such premature demonstrations." Nevertheless, in his reply to the Harrison Corresponding Committee, he indicated his support of the nominations.[36]

On October 5, three hundred Harrison supporters in New York City celebrated the anniversary of the battle of the Thames with a festival and dinner at Niblo's Saloon, a popular gathering place on Broadway near Prince Street. An old Federalist, General Robert Bogardus, was president, and Gulian Verplanck and Alexander Hamilton, Jr., were members of the committee. Among the decorations was "a large transparency representing general Harrison leading the charge against the British and Indians, at the battle of the Thames." "This affair took place twenty odd years ago," remarked Philip Hone, "and this is the first time it has been celebrated in this part of the country; but as glorification is the order of the day, the Harrisonians thought it was better late than never." The Van Buren men held a dinner at Tammany Hall on the same day, with the Mayor presiding, in honor of *their* candidate for the vice-presidency, Colonel Richard M. Johnson of Kentucky, who had fought at the Thames and was said to have killed the great Indian warrior, Tecumseh. Among the regular and volunteer toasts, in which Johnson was frequently lauded, not a single man mentioned Harrison's name! "The play of Hamlet was performed, the part of Hamlet (by particular desire) left out," Hone quipped.[37]

Following their dinner, the Harrison Republican Committee called upon the General's friends throughout the state to appoint delegates to a nominating convention, which was to meet at Albany on the first Wednesday in February 1836. But the patrician Hone, for one, would not commit himself to Harrison, White, or any other man until it was quite certain that Webster had no chance. As he wrote in his diary:

> Daniel Webster's claim is incomparably stronger than that of either of the other candidates. He is entitled to the people's votes, for he is their true friend, and not the friend of a party or a section. He merits the support of his country, for his patriotism

is not of those scanty proportions which will cover only a part of his country, and the Constitution can never be so safe in any other hands as in his who has proved himself its ablest expounder and firmest supporter. I go, therefore, for Webster until it is made manifest that he has no chance of success, and then for the next best man, Harrison or whoever it may be.[38]

The *New-York American* urged Webster's friends in the city to give public evidence of their support for his candidacy. On October 27, it editorialized: "The time for such expression is now come, and we may assume . . . that some pretty decisive movement will soon be made in this city, by the friends of Daniel Webster and the Constitution." Yet a month went by before a notice was published in the *American* with 1,100 signatures: "Liberty and Union, now and forever, one and inseparable. The citizens of the city and county of New York, friendly to the election of *Daniel Webster* to the Presidency, are requested to assemble at Masonic Hall, on Friday evening, the 4th of December." The large meeting adopted resolutions endorsing Webster's candidacy and appointed an executive committee of thirty to correspond with his friends in other states with a view to furthering his election. But, significantly, no state nominating convention was called. The meeting was a grand gesture and nothing more. Even loyal Hone had abandoned hope; he now suggested that in the end, Harrison, White, and Webster would "give up their own *ground* and take to *Clay*."[39] It was a bad pun and a worse prediction.

## NOTES

*1.* Washington *National Intelligencer,* January 27, 1835, quoting Philadelphia *National Gazette,* n.d.; Salmon P. Chase to S. F. Vinton, February, 1835, quoted in Robert B. Warden, *An Account of the Private Life and Public Services of Salmon Portland Chase* (Cincinnati, 1874), p. 248.

*2.* Seward to Thurlow Weed, January 27, 1835, quoted in Seward, *Autobiography,* p. 250.

*3.* Niles' *Weekly Register,* XLVIII (1835), 248, quoting Baltimore *Patriot,* n.d.

*4.* Stanwood, *History of the Presidency,* pp. 182-183; Joseph Howard Parks,

*John Bell of Tennessee* (Baton Rouge, 1950), p. 108; *Niles' Weekly Register*, XLIX (1835), 384.

*5.* Clay is quoted in John Vollmer Mering, *The Whig Party in Missouri* (Columbia, 1967), pp. 32-33.

*6.* Washington *National Intelligencer*, July 8, September 30, 1835.

*7.* Washington *Globe*, June 4, 30, July 15, 1835.

*8.* Bailhache to Henry Clay, July 8, 1835, quoted in Reed, "Emergence of the Whig Party in the North," p. 367.

*9.* Clay to [John Bailhache], July 14, 1835, *Works of Clay*, V, 394.

*10.* Seward to Thurlow Weed, February 15, 1835, quoted in Reed, "Emergence of the Whig Party in the North," p. 305.

*11.* Seward to Thurlow Weed, March 15, 1835, *ibid.*, pp. 305-306.

*12.* Quoted in Fuess, *Daniel Webster*, II, 42.

*13.* Arthur M. Schlesinger, Jr., *The Age of Jackson* (Boston, 1946), p. 279.

*14.* Samuel F. Vinton to Salmon P. Chase, February 8, 1835, quoted in Warden, *Life of Chase*, pp. 246-247.

*15.* Dorothy Burne Goebel, *William Henry Harrison, a Political Biography. Indiana Historical Collections*, Vol. XIV (Indianapolis, 1926), p. 306.

*16.* Seward, *Autobiography*, pp. 252, 265.

*17.* Harrison to General Soloman Van Rensselaer, January 15, 1835, quoted in Mrs. Catharina V. R. Bonney, *A Legacy of Historical Gleanings* (Albany, 1875), II, 55-56.

*18.* Webster to Edward Everett, July 2, 1835, Edward Everett Papers, Massachusetts Historical Society, Boston. (Hereafter cited as Everett Papers.); Freeman Cleaves, *Old Tippecanoe: William Henry Harrison and His Time* (New York, 1939), p. 295; Washington *United States Telegraph*, April 21, 1835; Washington *National Intelligencer*, July 21, 1835, quoting Cincinnati *Whig*, n.d.

*19.* Cleaves, *Old Tippecanoe*, pp. 296-297.

*20.* Washington *National Intelligencer*, September 30, 1835, quoting Louisville *Journal*, n.d.

*21.* Biddle to Herman Cope, August 11, 1835, *Biddle Correspondence*, p. 256.

*22.* Cope to Nicholas Biddle, September 2, 1835, Biddle Papers.

*23.* Washington *United States Telegraph*, August 12, 1835; *New-York American*, September 18, 1835, quoting Cincinnati *Gazette*, September 7, 1835.

*24.* Washington *National Intelligencer*, September 30, October 28, 1835, quoting Pittsburgh *Advocate*, n.d.; Boston *Daily Atlas*, August 31, 1835.

*25.* *New-York American*, August 28, 1835; Boston *Daily Atlas*, August 31, 1835.

*26.* Albany *Argus*, August 14, 1835; *Niles' Weekly Register*, XLIX (1835), 19, 88-89, 106; Joseph Williamson, "Daniel Webster's Visit to Maine in 1835," *Historical Magazine*, XIX (1871), 11-13; *Writings and Speeches*, II, 159-165.

*27.* Washington *National Intelligencer*, November 2, 1835; *Writings and Speeches*, II, 175-186.

*28.* Washington *National Intelligencer,* November 3, 1835, quoting *New-York American,* n.d.

*29.* Elisha Whittlesey to Daniel Webster, September 14, 1833, Webster Papers.

*30.* Webster to James Brooks, August 5, 1834, *Writings and Speeches,* XVI, 241-242.

*31.* Webster to Daniel Webster, September 6, 1834, in Harry R. Warfel (ed.), *Letters of Noah Webster* (New York, 1953), p. 433.

*32.* Plumer, "Reminiscences of Daniel Webster," *Writings and Speeches,* XVII, 558.

*33.* Elisha Whittlesey to Daniel Webster, September 14, 1833, Webster Papers.

*34.* Webster to James H. Bingham, August 24, 1835, *Writings and Speeches,* XVIII, 11.

*35.* Washington *National Intelligencer,* July 11, 1835.

*36.* *Niles' Weekly Register,* XLIX (1835), 36; Seward to Thurlow Weed, September 8, 1835, quoted in Reed, "Emergence of the Whig Party in the North," p. 307.

*37.* *Niles' Weekly Register,* XLIX (1835), 133-134; Tuckerman, *Hone Diary,* I, 166.

*38.* Washington *National Intelligencer,* October 28, 1835; Tuckerman, *Hone Diary,* I, 172.

*39.* *Niles' Weekly Register,* XLIX (1835), 133-134, 241; Washington *National Intelligencer,* October 28, 1835; *New-York American,* October 27, December 5, 1835; Tuckerman, *Hone Diary,* I, 166, 172.

# PENNSYLVANIA DECIDES THE CONTEST

**7** Whig leaders, meanwhile, were looking to Pennsylvania, with its big bloc of thirty electoral votes, to designate the Whig candidate in the North. Henry Clay concluded that if the Keystone State would give "satisfactory demonstrations" of support for Harrison, it would be expedient to run him as the most available candidate against Van Buren. "The issue of the Rhode Island election following that of Connecticut, proves, I fear, that it is vain to look even to New England for the support of Mr. Webster."[1] Other party leaders echoed the Kentuckian. James Barbour of Virginia wrote to Clay: ". . . we have no prospect of excluding Van, but by the plan you suggest of selecting two candidates that will be strongest in their respective sections. White, I apprehend for the South, Webster, for the East, North and West, or whomsoever Pennsylvania prefers—for in my view she holds the election in her hands."[2] Biddle agreed. His prescription: "This disease [Jacksonianism] is to be treated as a local disorder—apply local remedies—if Genl. Harrison will run better than any body else in Pennsa., by all means unite upon him! That as far as I understand the case, is the feeling very generally of the opposition. . . ."[3]

Harrison's campaign in Pennsylvania began on January 19, 1835, when a "Democratic Republican" public meeting at Harrisburg nominated him "as the Democratic candidate of the people for the next Presidency."[4] Coldly received at first, Harrison's candidacy gained momentum during the spring and summer. Nicholas Biddle assured Herman Cope that there was every willingness on the part of the Whigs in the state to give the General "fair play," and promised that "if our friends are satisfied that he can get more votes in Pennsa than any other candidate of the opposition they will take him up cheerfully & support him cordially."[5] Harrison himself thought his prospects in the state were excellent. "I am persuaded . . . that a general declaration for me by the Whigs & Anti-masons of your state would at once put Webster *hors de combat*," he advised a Pennsylvania supporter. To John Tipton, he wrote on October 9 that "My *progress* has been such as not only to excite my gratitude but my astonishment. You may rely upon it that Pennsylvania will give me a most triumphant majority."[6]

By September, Harrison men in Pennsylvania were reporting a "very strong interest for the old Genl" in that state and in Maryland. The friends of Joseph Ritner, the Antimasonic-Whig candidate for governor were saying, "elect him and the state is safe for the opposition and that Genl Harrison is the man to beat Van in this state. . . ."[7] G. B. Trevor, a Philadelphia Whig, reported on September 12 that "the manner in which Genl Harrison appears to be making headway in the Keystone State is very similar to that in which Genl Jackson's popularity commenced. Neither the political leaders nor the newspapers appear to be as yet much in his favor but to any person who watches the current of public opinion, it must be very evident that a strong tide is setting in his favor among the great body of the people." Trevor admitted that his first choice was Henry Clay, but as he seemed to be out of the question, he would go for Harrison as the "most available" candidate to defeat Van Buren. He predicted a victory for Ritner in the gubernatorial contest, and promised that after the election, meetings would be held in Philadelphia and other large towns in the state to take up Harrison for the presidency. "That we can carry him in Pennsylvania against Van Buren I will not permit myself to doubt. There is as you know a tide in the affairs of men which taken at the flood leads on to fortune. That flood is now setting in; the tide which is bearing the Genl at present into popular favor is steady and increasing."[8]

By November, there were sixty-five Harrison papers in Pennsylvania; and his prospects were sufficiently bright to permit a group calling itself the "Democratic Republican Committee" to issue a call for the Harrison men to meet in convention at Harrisburg on December 14, to frame an electoral ticket and to make plans to secure his election. It was stated that "the Democratic supporters of the present chief magistrate, the Democratic Whigs, and the Democratic Anti-Masons may, without losing their party names, or giving up their party organizations, be cordially invited to participate."[9]

To meet the Harrison challenge, Webster's friends conceived a campaign strategy adapted to the peculiar political situation existing within the state. Although the Antimasonic party was disintegrating and merging with the Whigs in most states, in Pennsylvania it remained the major party in opposition to the dominant Democrats. The Whigs were a minor third party. Antimasonry had a broad appeal in predominantly German areas in the southeast where there were strong religious sects committed firmly to tenets forbidding oaths and in the Scotch-Irish counties in the southwest. The movement combined an attack on the Masonic Order and opposition to the state administration's canal policy with a general hostility to the Democratic party. The Whigs made an overture for an alliance against the Jackson men but were coolly received. A Young Men's Whig Association of Pittsburgh, formed just before the congressional election of 1834, denied any feelings of animosity toward the Antimasons as a party, and declared "that the attempt made by some of the *violent leaders* of that party, to identify the Whigs with the Masonic Institution is equally at variance with *truth* and *common sense.*"[10]  However, in 1835 the two parties joined in supporting Joseph Ritner, of Washington County, the Antimasonic candidate for governor. The broadbeamed and good natured Ritner was the son of poor German immigrants and enjoyed great popularity in the German counties. Nominated by the Antimasons for governor in 1829, he was defeated by 16,000 votes. Re-nominated in 1832, he lost the governorship by only 3,000 votes, while Jackson was carrying the state by a majority exceeding 25,000.

In 1835 a split in the Democratic ranks between the friends of the conservative governor, George Wolf, and the more progressive Henry A. Muhlenberg, the "Wolves" and the "Mules," gave "Ritner the Farmer" the election by a decisive plurality. The vote was 94,023 for Ritner, 65,805 for Wolf, and 40,586 for Muhlenberg. Ritner carried traditional Antimasonic counties and the Whig strongholds of Pittsburgh and Philadelphia. The Antimasonic-Whig coalition gained a majority of seats in the lower house of the state legislature, and although holdovers permitted the Democrats to retain the Senate, the Coalition could control on joint ballot.[11]

Any Whig presidential candidate who hoped to carry Pennsylvania in 1836 would have to satisfy the state's Antimasons that he was sound on the Masonic question; for if the Antimasons nominated their own candidate, the opposition vote would be split and Van Buren would win easily in what might prove to be the decisive state in the election. Further complicating the situation was the existence of two rival elements, the radical "Exclusives" and the moderate "Coalitionists," within the Antimasonic ranks. Among the Exclusive leaders were such party veterans as Thaddeus Stevens of Lancaster and Congressman Harmar Denny of Pittsburgh. The Exclusives were opposed to a formal association with the Whigs, which some of the Coalitionists were urging in order to control the legislature and the patronage, but were willing to hold out the olive branch to the Muhlenberg Democrats. They interpreted Ritner's victory as an opportunity to expose Masonry and to abolish oaths and secret orders, to restore economy in government, and cut taxes. Early in 1836 Stevens declared there was "no other question than Masonry and Anti-Masonry."[12] The Exclusives also favored the calling of a national convention to nominate candidates for President and Vice-President; Coalitionists opposed it, prefering to find candidates acceptable to the Whigs.

Webster and his friends set out to woo the Antimasons of Pennsylvania, confident that once their support had been won, the Whigs in the state must either accept Webster or face certain defeat.[13] Also, support for his candidacy was sought on the ground that he stood the best chance of uniting the anti-Van Buren men in the North, and Webster needed the Pennsylvania Antimasons behind him to make good on that claim. During the Senate debate on the removal of the deposits, Webster swore that he knew of no body of citizens in the country, "whose principles and opinions, on all its leading interests, are more thoroughly sound and patriotic, than those of the Antimasons of Pennsylvania." Although the party had a distinct object of its own constantly in view, it had always showed itself "unwavering and steadfast in its attachment to the Constitution, in its maintenance of the authority of law, in its love of liberty, and in its support of the great interests and true policy of the country."[14]

Webster chose Edward Everett to conduct the secret negotiations with the Pennsylvania Antimasons; as the joint gubernatorial candidate of the Antimasons and Whigs of Massachusetts, he was a particularly suitable choice. Thaddeus Stevens enjoyed a reputation as the great Antimasonic leader in the Keystone State, and was expected to handle Governor Ritner, who was supposedly a simple-hearted man. Everett therefore opened a correspondence with him on the question of the presidency. He asked Stevens: "Will not the glorious result of your gubernatorial election infuse new life into the Anti Van Buren party in Penna. and will not our Antimasonic friends see their way clear to take the lead in a movement in favor of Mr. Webster?" An article in the Pittsburgh *Times* of October 14, the first of a series on the presidential election, had suggested that Webster was so situated that he would probably not now accept an Antimasonic nomination. Everett assured Stevens that "I know of no ground for this opinion," and feared it was founded on "sinister efforts" to sow discord between the Antimasons and Webster's other friends. Finally, he begged the Pennsylvanian to make a "free communication of your views, in entire confidence, if you wish it.—"[15]

To Governor-elect Ritner, Everett wrote that same day to express the satisfaction of Massachusetts Whigs at the result of the Pennsylvania election.

> I beg leave to assure you, that the liveliest interest has been taken in your election; & that it is considered as the most auspicious event, which has for a long time occurred in the political world. We look to it with cheerful & confident hope, as the forerunner of the political regeneration of the Country; and as an event, which will exert the happiest influence in placing Pensa. & Massts. side by side in the great national struggle which is approaching.[16]

But he did not confide in Ritner, as he had in Stevens.

Before committing himself to either Webster or Harrison, Stevens wanted a frank statement of their views on Masonry. In a letter to Harrison, Stevens asked two succinct questions: first, "Do you believe that Free Masonry and all other secret oath bound societies are evils and inconsistent with the genius and safety of Republican Government?" and second, "Will you join your Anti-Masonic fellow citizens in the use of all constitutional, fair and honorable means for their final and effectual suppression?"[17]

The General replied that while he believed in Antimasonic principles and considered the evils arising from Masonry as a proper subject for "the deliberations and actions of some constituted authorities of the country," yet he was certain that there was no power to extinguish Masonry, "either in the whole Government of the United States or in any of its Departments, and that an attempt to exercise it would constitute a usurpation of power, pregnant if tolerated by the people with mischiefs infinitely more fatal than those which it was intended to remedy."[18]

This bold reply was gall and wormwood to the fiery Stevens. On the other hand, Webster's reply through Everett to a similar inquiry proved more agreeable. In reply to Stevens' query:

"Will Mr. W. if addressed on the subject avow himself an Anti-mason?" Everett, after consulting with Webster, assured him that "his answer to any communication, which you would sanction on that subject, would be satisfactory." Webster was ready to reaffirm his favorable opinion of the political sentiments and principles of the Antimasons of Pennsylvania which he had earlier expressed in the Senate; to announce his entire approval of their sentiments, in as far as he understood them, in regard to secret societies; and to reaffirm his approval of the act of the Massa-chusetts legislature abolishing all secret oaths. ". . . if the above sketch is not what you would think desirable," Everett added, "let me know in confidence, by what alterations or additions it can be made so." He predicted that if Webster received a nomina-tion from the National Anti-Masonic Convention, he would be certain to carry Pennsylvania, Vermont, Massachusetts, Rhode Island, Delaware, Maryland, Kentucky, and Louisiana, while Connecticut and the states of the Old Northwest (at least Ohio and Indiana) would be debatable ground. In any event, Van Buren would be defeated, and the entire credit would go to the Antimasonic party, since without their lead nothing could be done.[19]

Stevens did not think highly of Webster as a candidate; and shortly before writing Everett, he had conceded that the Senator could not take Pennsylvania from Van Buren and that Harrison was the only man who could defeat the New Yorker. In a letter to John B. Wallace he maintained that by postponing action upon the presidency the Antimasons could force a delay in the choice of an opponent for Van Buren, since without the Anti-masonic vote no candidate could win. If they should find that Van Buren could not be beaten, they could go their own way. "But if Antimasons are to nominate a man with whom they can not succeed, they will nominate a distinctive Antimason—so as to keep their party inflexibly together, and compel other parties to adopt our principles or endure perpetual defeat. The destruc-tion of Masonry is an object which we shall not lose sight of either in success or defeat."[20]

Stevens even asked Everett if *he* would accept an Antimasonic nomination, but the latter, while gratefully acknowledging this suggestion, replied that as Webster's political and personal friend, and "the depository of his most confidential counsils [sic]," he could not permit himself to "intercept" the support of the Pennsylvania Antimasons or any other support, which could be gained for him.[21] The enigmatic Stevens then resolved to go for Webster and to carry his party along with him. Some of the Pennsylvania Antimasons began to mention Stevens himself as their candidate for Vice-President on a national Antimasonic ticket; and Stevens no doubt found this idea acceptable. The Gettysburg *Star,* which he had founded, nominated him on a Webster slate.[22]

Just when things looked promising in his negotiations with the Pennsylvania Antimasons, Everett was embarrassed by a serious rift between the Whigs and Antimasons in Massachusetts growing out of John Quincy Adams' defeat for the United States Senate. In excluding Adams, the Webster Whigs had been too clever by half. Massachusetts Antimasons were indignant that Webster had used his influence against Adams and held him chiefly responsible for the old man's embarrassment. They stated that when the decision in the House was in doubt, "a prominent member of the Boston delegation took some papers from his pocket, waved them in triumph over his head . . . declaring them to be letters from Washington *of the highest authority,* unfavorable to Mr. Adams." Taking advantage of this discontent, Benjamin Hallett, editor of the Boston *Advocate,* used Adams' defeat as a pretext to desert Webster's candidacy and to swing Antimasonic support to Van Buren. Charles Francis Adams, still sore at his father's defeat, encouraged Hallett. It was an opportunity, he felt, "to pay off some old scores besides doing what I believe the only advisable thing." The *Advocate* accused Whig leaders of using Webster as a stalking horse against Van Buren in the interest of Hugh Lawson White, and piously claimed to have more respect for Webster's merits than those "who are resolved on sacrificing him without his consent in a hopeless contest, merely to spite Martin Van Buren." With the contest reduced to a choice of Van Buren or White, the *Advocate* urged that all good Antimasons support the *northern* candidate, Van Buren.[23]

Hallett's actions alarmed the Webster Whigs, for the *Advocate* was an influential journal, not only among the Antimasons of Massachusetts, but in other states. Its editorial policy could undermine Webster's hopes of securing their support. Edward Everett hastened to assure Stevens and Harmar Denny that the *Advocate's* position did not represent the true attitude of the Massachusetts Antimasons. The split between Webster and Adams had originated in "misinformation & exaggeration," he wrote to Denny, had been aggravated by persons hostile to Webster, and had been seized upon by Hallett as a pretext to desert him, under pretense of espousing Adams' cause, "but in reality for the sake of giving the State to Van Buren." If the state's Antimasons were polled, nine-tenths would go for Webster; but Adams' feelings toward him were irrecoverably alienated. Everett admitted to Stevens that all movements upon the part of Massachusetts Antimasons in Webster's behalf had been "paralyzed" by Hallett's actions.

> He has made up his mind to go for V.B. & conducts his paper with great adroitness & skill so as to take the antimasons with him, in that course. He has nothing to alledge [sic] as the ground for his opposition to Mr. W. but a pretended hostility of Mr. W. to Mr. Adams:—which were it founded in truth would seem rather a poor reason for selling the Antimasonic party to V.B.[24]

Denny had already divined Hallett's purpose. "I think I perceive that Mr. Haller [sic] of Boston is adroitly endeavoring to place our party in a position by which we will be compelled to vote for Van B. or our opposition to him paralyzed," he wrote. "The movement is coming but I think it will not succeed. It is to reduce the contest to V.B. & White." Denny was thoroughly in sympathy with Webster's candidacy and favored his nomination by a national Antimasonic convention with either Thaddeus Stevens or Amos Ellmaker for Vice-President. The prospect of carrying such a ticket, he thought "very favorable."[25]

The Pennsylvania Antimasons were to hold a state convention at Harrisburg on December 14, 1835, and Webster's friends in the party wanted this meeting to nominate him for the presidency as a preliminary to his nomination by the national convention.

The national gathering was originally scheduled to meet in Washington on the last Monday in December 1835, unless the National Antimasonic Committee advised otherwise. After consultation with the several state committees, the National Committee agreed to move the meeting from Washington to either New York or Philadelphia and to delay it until an unspecified date in the spring of 1836. The exact time and place were to be decided upon at "no distant day."[26]

On November 11, 1835, the Antimasons of Allegheny County met in Pittsburgh to select delegates to the Harrisburg convention. All candidates nominated pledged themselves to Webster, and resolutions were passed with but one dissenting vote instructing those chosen to urge his nomination at the state convention. Five delegates were selected: Neville Craig, Harmar Denny, Benjamin Darlington, William W. Irwin, and J. C. Gilleland. The Webster press in Pennsylvania hailed these proceedings as evidence of his popularity with the Antimasons of western Pennsylvania and predicted Antimasons throughout the state would follow their example. "This is a small beginning," Denny wrote to Webster, "but I hope [it] will be the basis of more important and extended action."[27]

To bring the Pennsylvania Antimasons to Webster's standard, the Allegheny County delegates requested a letter from him expressing his views on the subject of secret societies which they could make public at once.[28] Webster's reply was a clear appeal for Antimasonic support. He avowed his entire accordance with the opinions of their party, "so far as I understand them," on secret societies. Masonry was "essentially wrong" in the principles of its formation and from its very nature liable to great abuses. Under the influence of this conviction, he had heartily approved the Massachusetts law abolishing secret oaths and obligations. Finally, he affirmed that he had "ever found the antimasons of Pennsylvania true to the Constitution, to the Union, and to the great interests of the country."[29]

When Webster's reply reached Pittsburgh, it was opened by William W. Irwin, who immediately wrote back suggesting some "slight modifications." Since the opinions of the Antimasons of

Pennsylvania on the subject of Masonry had been repeatedly expressed for at least six years, Irwin feared that Webster's phrase "so far as I understand them" in reference to these principles might offend some of the Antimasons in the state. He therefore suggested that these words be struck out. Irwin also thought that since some Massachusetts Antimasons had expressed doubt as to the efficacy of that state's law against secret oaths in suppressing Masonry, "it would be prudent to make no mention of that law." In its place, he suggested: "Under the influence of this conviction, it is my opinion that future administration of all such oaths and obligations should be prohibited by law." "With these slight alterations," Irwin concluded blandly, "I trust that your letter will be as satisfactory to every anti-mason in Pennsylvania, and throughout the Union, as I take pleasure in assuring you it has proved to . . . myself."[30] Infected with the presidential virus, the "Godlike Daniel" humbly submitted to this censorship by a local politician and made the suggested changes.[31]

The Pennsylvania State Antimasonic Committee also addressed a letter to Webster requesting his views on Masonry. He referred them to his letter to the Allegheny County delegates as indicative of his general views on the subject, but added that there could be no question of the constitutional right of those who believed secret societies to be either moral or political evils, "to seek the removal of such evils, by the exercise of the elective franchise, as well as by other lawful means."[32]

The Antimasons wished to know if patronage would be given them should Webster be elected President. The harrassed candidate wrote to William W. Irwin that while it did not consist with his sense of duty to hold out such promises on the eve of a great election, "I hope no one hesitates to believe that I am altogether incapable of disappointing, in that respect, any natural and just expectations which friends may form."[33]

Earlier, in April 1835, the State Antimasonic Committee had written General Harrison requesting a "candid and explicit" statement of his sentiments on Masonry. The old soldier shocked the committee by denying any knowledge of the principles of the Antimasonic party in Pennsylvania, "otherwise than they are opposed to masonry." He indicated that if elected President he would not discriminate against Masons in his public conduct, and declared that if Masonry was an evil, it would only be corrected "by public opinion, by the people themselves, and not by their agents, and least of all those who administer the government of the United States."[34] Harrison had thus boldly denied the very foundation of political Antimasonry, and the State Committee, fearful the reply would injure Ritner's candidacy, suppressed it until after the election. In October it was made public and according to Irwin, gave "very great offense" to many Antimasons throughout the state.[35] The Webster press was overjoyed with Harrison's letter. The Pittsburgh *Gazette* predicted it would cut him off from all hope of support by the Antimasons of Pennsylvania: "Its publication *verbatim* and *liberatim,* with orthographical errors, shows that he is not in favor." Denny and Everett congratulated themselves that the possibility of his receiving Antimasonic backing was over. Everett wrote to Stevens that "Genl. Harrison's prospects . . . will as far as the A.M. party is concerned, be seriously affected by his letter of the 6th of May to Messes Wallace & Shock."[36]

A Jackson triumph in eight of the fifteen districts in the fall Ohio election gave the Webster papers an occasion to tag Harrison with the "unavailability" label. The General tried to explain the Whig defeat in his own district. "Our house was divided against itself." No organization or committee of vigilance existed and the ticket had been named by a clique which he disowned. As a result, fewer than 1,500 Whigs had voted in Cincinnati, a city of 31,000 people.[37] But the Pittsburgh *Advocate* declared that the failure of the Whig cause in Ohio was directly due to Harrison's nomination. The warrior candidate was a mere " 'will o' the wisp,' " who would dance about for a week or two and then go down in darkness. When the Pennsylvania Antimasons and Whigs declared against him, Ohio would abandon him.[38]

The Webster journals reasserted *their* candidate's availability. The "vast majority" of the eastern states supported him, declared the Philadelphia *National Gazette,* including the major part of the Whigs and Antimasons of the Keystone State. The Boston *Courier* ridiculed the idea that the White and Harrison papers could drive Webster from the field; "could they reduce the Alle-gaghanies [sic] to a level with the prairies, or compel the Potomac to change its course and throw its waters into Lake Superior or Hudson's Bay, by a few newspaper paragraphs, they might hope, by the same means to induce Mr. Webster to withdraw himself." The *Courier* complained that probably no man ever suffered more than Webster had from the "pains taken by his *professed friends,* to convince the public that he was not *available.*"[39]

While courting the Pennsylvania Antimasons, Everett, at the same time, was trying to retain the allegiance of the state's Whig minority. Many members of the party felt that Webster like Clay was no longer available. Early in the year McLean had been told that "Webster's nomination tempts all the old federalists & the bank papers are evidently his, but intelligent politicians will not dream of carrying him."[40] Everett fought a delaying action to prevent the Whigs in Pennsylvania from bolting to Harrison, confident that once Webster was given the Antimasonic nomina-tion, they would be forced to sustain him or accept inevitable de-feat. As he explained to Nathan Sargent: "It seems to me, that Mr. W's whig friends in Penna. have no prospect of success, but in acting in continued concert with the Anti-masons: if the latter do not emphatically disclaim the support of Genl. H, I shall be disappointed."[41] When the Harrison party in Philadelphia called a public meeting for November 9, 1835, to endorse his candidacy and select delegates to the Harrison convention at Harrisburg, Everett was fearful it portended the General's nomination by Webster's Whig "friends" in the city. He warned Nicholas Biddle that any Whig movement for Harrison would be premature since it was unlikely the Antimasons would second it.

> This being the case, would not our Whig friends find themselves not a little embarrassed, with a nomination of Genl. H. on their hands?—That nomination not being concurred in by the Anti-masons, could it have any other conceivable effect than to give the state to Van B?—Why should our Whig friends at this crisis move against Mr. Webster? Cui Bono?[42]

The Harrison meeting was held as scheduled but was not a success. The *National Gazette* pronounced it a "miscarriage," attributable to the fact that the great majority of the Whigs in the city immeasurably preferred Webster to the General.[43] However, Biddle explained the outcome of the meeting more fully to Everett. For some time, he stated candidly, "our friends" had regarded Webster's election "as an impracticable good for which it was vain to contend," and had been disposed to unite with other portions of the opposition in the support of any candidate of less merit, but with better chances of success. It was understood in Philadelphia that the Antimasonic party would nominate Harrison, that they would be joined by many malcontents from the Jackson party, and the addition of the Whigs to these, it was thought, would secure a triumph over Van Buren. The Harrison meeting had been called under this impression, and all appearances indicated it would be a large one—when, two days before it was to take place, an officer of the Bank, Mr. Cowperthwait, arrived in town from the West. He said he had recently seen Henry Clay and many of the Antimasonic and Whig leaders of the interior of the state, that Clay was "very decided" in his preference for Webster, and that the opposition in the interior, especially the Antimasons, would support Webster but not Harrison. This intelligence made a "strong impression" and gave a new aspect to the meeting, so that all that was to be inferred from it was a willingness to support Harrison but an equal willingness to unite on another candidate. "In the meantime the antimasons are preparing to nominate that other," Biddle concluded, "& from what I understand from the conversation of Mr. Stevens with myself & with others, that candidate will certainly not be Genl. Harrison & probably will be Mr. Webster. The result is, as I understand it, that the meeting has had no injurious effect, & that they who attended it, are willing to follow any other lead which promises success."[44]

Meanwhile, Whigs friendly to Webster's candidacy held meetings to demonstrate their support. On November 7, the Whigs of Allegheny County met in Pittsburgh, endorsed him; recommended that his friends throughout the state meet in convention at Harris-

burg on January 4, 1836, to form an electoral ticket and nominate a candidate for Vice-President; and selected five delegates
to represent the county at the convention. A corresponding committee of nineteen members was appointed to write Webster's
friends throughout the state and nation. In the eastern part of
the state, a meeting in Wilkes-Barre (November 21) adopted
resolutions in favor of his candidacy. The Wyoming *Herald*
declared that it had been a long time "since we have seen so many
grey-headed [political] veterans together on such an occasion."
In Philadelphia, the Webster Whigs were summoned by an anon-
ymous notice in the city's papers to a preparatory meeting at the
Court House on November 18. When the citizens gathered, they
discovered that no arrangements had been made for a meeting.
Moving to the Bolivar House the group organized and a committee was appointed to make preparations for a general town
meeting. Held on November 25, the gathering invited Webster
to attend a complimentary dinner in the city, but took no other
action—an indication that the Philadelphia Whigs had already
abandoned him, the dinner being intended as a compensatory
gesture.[45]

At this time Harrison's friends in the state were making
frantic efforts to correct the poor impression made on the Antimasonic party by his letter of May 6 to the State Antimasonic
Committee. William Ayres of the Pennsylvania legislature gently
explained to the General that his views on Masonry had been
misunderstood. His letter had been construed to mean that it
was unconstitutional for the people to use the ballot box "for
the suppression of what they deem dangerous to equal rights" or
to "instruct their agents to perform what they themselves have a
right to do." Ayres assured Harrison that the Antimasons were
not warring on Masons as individuals but on the Masonic institution. They did not desire that the power of the federal government, or any of its departments, should be used to suppress
Masonry, but that the President's appointive power should be
used to deny office to anyone who put their Masonic obligations
above their duty to civil society and to the laws of the country.
Would Harrison give his views on these subjects?[46]

Harrison would. He was at a loss to conceive upon what fair principle of construction his letter could have been construed as a denunciation of the Antimasonic party. Certainly the people had the right both to form associations to correct abuses not immediately cognizable by law and to instruct their agents. While the federal government had no right to interfere with the party principles or movements of the people in cases where the law was not violated, it was the duty of the appointing power to inquire strictly into the principles of those who were applicants for office.

> For my own part, [said Harrison] I hesitate not to say, that I would as soon think of appointing to an office under this republic, one of the sprigs of English nobility—a scion from the pure tory stock of the house of Eldon, or Lowthes, or Jenkinson, or Wellesley, as an American citizen who would asset his right to enter into an Engagement or Combination, which would release him from paramount obligations of duty to the Constitution and Laws of his country.47

This letter to Ayres, while unacceptable to the radical Antimasons of Pennsylvania, was elastic enough to satisfy the more pragmatic Antimasonic leaders.

December brought the Harrison-Webster struggle in the Keystone State to a climax. Both the Harrison and Antimasonic conventions were to meet in Harrisburg on December 14, 1835, with public attention centering on the latter. Most observers gave Harrison the edge for the Antimasonic nomination. "At present the friends of Webster and Harrison are carrying on a pretty spirited contest for the nomination . . . at Harrisburgh [sic]," reported an Ohio congressman. "It is doubtful which will be nominated although I am inclined to think it will be Harrison."48 A correspondent of the Boston *Daily Advertiser* in Washington wrote that "the rumor grows constant, that General Harrison is to be nominated for the Presidency by the Pennsylvanians now in Convention."49

Still, the Webster Whigs remained confident. Caleb Cushing thought Harrison was "sheer naught," and that "Neither his intellectual character nor his general habits can give him vogue

at the North."[50]  He penned a most flattering biographical sketch
of Webster, which appeared in the *National Intelligencer* on
December 2, 1835, in time to be read by the delegates at Harrisburg.  Webster was highly pleased with the sketch and wrote
Cushing from New York City that it was "much read & talked
about here."  He suggested that one thing more might "with
truth" be added about the War of 1812, something like:

> In the recess of Congress, in the summer of 1814, when the whole
> seaboard was threatened by investigation, Mr. W. gave the prin-
> cipal part of his time in cooperating with others for preparing
> for defense, in case of an attack by the enemy in his neighborhood.
> By the citizens of Portsmouth, & on the nomination of that
> venerable republican, John Langdon, he was placed at the head
> of the principal committee raised to concert means of defense,
> & he offered his personal services to the Governor of the State,
> to be commanded in any mode in which they might be thought
> useful.[51]

Webster himself evidently considered his prospects in Pennsylvania to be very favorable.  Hone dined with him on December
8 in New York City at the home of Charles March and had never
seen him so agreeable; "for five hours he was the life of the company; cheerful, gay, full of anecdotes, and entirely free from the
sort of gloomy abstraction in which I have sometimes seen him,
as it were, envelop himself."[52]

Webster's frank sympathy for Antimasonic principles had
brought Thaddeus Stevens around to his support; but this proved
to be a mixed blessing.  The ambitious Stevens had opposed the
nomination of Joseph Ritner for governor, and now was seeking
to control his administration.  Honest and intelligent but of a
trusting nature, Ritner permitted the Lancaster "high priest of
Antimasonry" to shape some of the most objectionable features
of his administration, although he always denied it.[53]  Now, in a
gesture of independence, Ritner defied Stevens and threw his
influence and patronage behind Harrison's candidacy.  While
traveling to Harrisburg as Governor-elect, he had shared a railroad car with Clay, who was on his way to Washington, and the

Kentuckian probably urged on him the wisdom and policy of supporting the General.[54]

When the Antimasonic convention met in Harrisburg on December 14, the fight between the two factions broke out on the convention floor. In a trial of strength over the seating of a contested delegate, James Todd, Ritner's nominee for attorney-general, the Ritner-backed Coalitionists defeated the pro-Webster Exclusives led by Stevens. Realizing that Harrison would receive a nomination if it should come to a vote, the Exclusives tried to refer the nomination of candidates to the national convention, but were voted down, ninety-eight to thirty-six. At that point, Stevens and eight other delegates, including Harmar Denny, the chairman of the convention, read a formal protest and stalked from the hall. The moderates then reorganized, placed Joseph Lawrence in the chair, and preceeded to make nominations for President and Vice-President. The next day, the convention named Harrison for President on the first ballot, giving him eighty-nine votes to twenty-nine for Webster, and chose Francis Granger of New York for Vice-President by acclamation. These nominations were seconded by the Harrison convention, which had adjourned from day to day while it waited for the Antimasonic body to act.[55]

The seceders, who the *National Intelligencer* declared to be "the bone and sinew of the Anti-Masonic party in Pennsylvania," refused to abide by the majority decision and issued a call for a national convention to meet in Philadelphia on May 4, 1836. In a public address, they charged that Ritner's attorney-general, James Todd, having persuaded his son to relinquish his seat in the convention to him, had used the "corrupt power of patronage" to swing the delegates to Harrison and to block the calling of a national convention. Sixty-four members of the convention were applicants for office; and in addition, twenty-four Whigs and one Mason had been among the delegates! The "Masonic Whig or Harrison convention" with which the Ritner forces had cooperated, had contained large numbers of adhering Masons as well as many "strenuous defenders" of the order. "It is firmly believed that every true Antimason in the State will refuse to sanction this coalition," said the seceders, "but hold himself bound by the decisions of the national convention about to be held."[56] Stevens wrote a letter to John Quincy Adams, enclosing his correspondence with Harrison, and asked Adams' opinion of the General's Antimasonry. "I have declined giving it," Adams noted primly in his diary, "because it was asked merely to operate against the nomination of Harrison, and I wish to avoid all interference with the election."[57]

Richard Rush of Philadelphia, an Antimasonic leader who had earlier gone over to the Democrats, wrote Van Buren that while Harrison's nomination had carried with it the "great body of antimasons of the state," as far as outward party signs indicated, and nearly all the Whigs outside of Philadelphia, "I am nevertheless well informed that besides the open seceders among the antimasons, there is uneasiness and discontent with a considerable class of them, at work inwardly." Rush proposed to fish in these troubled waters, to capture for the Democracy this class, as well as all those who were originally of that party. "I desire to see them where they ought all to be—with the great national cause as identified with the Baltimore nominations."[58]

Among the Antimasonic papers in Pennsylvania, only the Gettysburg *Star,* closely identified with Stevens, and the Pittsburgh *Times* seem to have supported the call for a national convention. The *Star* said that the meeting would "attempt to survive and sustain *pure unmixed* Anti-Masonry—not to daub over the foul treacherous doings of the 'base compound' Harrisburg Convention"; it would avoid "alike the insidious Masonic Van Buren and the unblushing Masonic Harrison." However, it proved a weak reed. Stevens and his friends passed strong resolutions condemning Harrison's nomination at Harrisburg and the role of the Whigs in effecting it, but the convention adjourned without nominating its own candidates.[59] A convention committee wrote Van Buren and Harrison asking if they would appoint "adhering Masons" to office. The Vice-President answered that whether an applicant was a Mason or an opponent of the order would not keep him from an office if otherwise qualified. Van

Buren's friends among the Pennsylvania Antimasons suppressed his letter. He was told that "it would be used against you by the Harrison men and would help you with no side." Harrison, in his reply, said he "would on no account nominate any man to office who held the opinion that his obligations to any secret society were superior to those which he avowed to the laws and constitution of his country."[60] Whether this dodge appeased Stevens and his friends was unclear. Harrison mentioned, in a private letter, the quarrel between the Pennsylvania Masons and the Antimasons, but did not refer to the quarrel within the Antimasonic party; "and there does not seem to be sufficient evidence on which to define Stevens' attitude between May and November, 1836."[61]

The Webster press bitterly denounced the Pennsylvania proceedings. The *National Intelligencer* questioned whether the votes of the two Harrisburg conventions had reflected "either the general sense of the Anti-masons, or of the Whigs . . . in the State." The Boston *Courier* warned that if Pennsylvania pursued the "mad and senseless career" marked out by the Harrisburg convention, "she will, perhaps, have the gratification of elevating to the Presidential Chair, Mr. Van Buren or Judge White."[62]

The Philadelphia *National Gazette* published a poem, "The Wigs Without a Cue," dedicated to the Harrisburg convention, which revealed clearly its disgust at Harrison's nomination. In the poem one *"Brigadier Humbug"* declares that to "gain the crowd" the Whigs must find a glorious hero for their candidate, and he knows just the man.

His name is *Harrison;* upon the banks
Of conscious Thames he played his warlike pranks,
And then a Gov'ner of North Western land
He held o'er Wolves and Indians wide command.
Upon the Senate floor, besides, he stood, and
talked of Rome, much to his country's good.
'Tis even said, to market he doth send
His corn and pigs, 'the Farmer of North Bend.'
With such a grand ballon [sic] he cannot fail
Direct into the *Mansion White* to sail.
You may depend sir, Martin will feel blue
When e'er we shout 'hurrah for *Tippecanoe.*'[63]

Webster's defeat in Pennsylvania was partially due to the feud between Ritner and Stevens; the Harrisburg *Chronicle* (a Van Buren paper) commented that Harrison's nomination "was as much intended to put down Thaddeus S. and a few others, as it was to put up General Harrison."[64] Yet, without this dispute, it is evident that the old soldier was considered the most available candidate by a majority of Whigs and Antimasons in the state, notwithstanding their regard for Webster's great talents.[65] According to Charles Miner, who was in Harrisburg while the conventions were in session, Webster's former association with the Federalist party had been an important cause of his defeat.

> What a farce! All agree, 'Mr. Webster is my first choice, but we cannot carry him.' Why? It seems strange that he who is the *first* choice of every one should be less popular than the man who is only the *second* choice, & confessedly his inferior. Ah, but he was a Federalist! Damning sin! Never to be forgiven: But he was opposed to the war![66]

The *Pennsylvania Reporter and Democratic Herald* had the most humorous if not the most profound explanation for Webster's defeat: "Mr. Webster has been fishing deep for the Antimasons of Pennsylvania, but the fish have slipped through his net."[67]

In Boston, Charles Francis Adams and Benjamin Hallett had been anxiously awaiting news from Harrisburg. Hallett, who according to Adams was "assailed from several quarters," expected Webster's nomination by the Antimasonic convention "Which brings the war into his own country." He had received letters from Everett protesting against the spirit with which he conducted the *Advocate,* and was very unwilling to "come to the mark" of attacking Webster, as Adams was insisting must be done if the course adopted by them was to be sustained. Calling at the *Advocate* office on December 21 for the latest news from Harrisburg, Adams was gratified to learn that the Antimasons were determined to support Harrison "and thus Mr. Webster is completely prostrated. Thus ends for the present a domination altogether too arbitrary to be submitted to with patience."[68]

However, after it became clear that Webster would not be a

serious candidate, the situation for a time became even more difficult for Adams. On December 26, Hallett called at Adams' home and visited for several hours, with the object of disclosing the result of an interview by request with Everett.

> It seems that the Pennsylvania nomination proves the death blow to the hopes of Mr. Webster. That under the indignation consequent upon it, as well as the sense of his own danger in perseverance, he and his friends wish now to come in under the shelter of Mr. Van Buren's influence—and that Mr. E. is anxious to make an effort to consolidate a party which made up of whigs and antimasons shall enable him to resist the decided attack that will next year be made upon him.

A letter had also been received from Henry Dana Ward, a member of the National Antimasonic Committee, very strongly intimating that the seceders from the Harrisburg convention friendly to Webster were disposed to take up Van Buren and for that end had nominated thirty-two delegates to the National Convention which the Committee had announced would take place in May at Philadelphia. Above all, the injunction was laid upon Hallett to say nothing against Webster as that might affect the plan.[69]

An alliance with the Webster Whigs would have been embarrassing for Adams, whose political involvement with Antimasonry had resulted from the treatment these very men had meted out to his father. As a result, he worked hard to prevent such a combination. He and Hallett agreed not to recognize the Pennsylvania delegation to the National Convention, since it did not represent the will or real opinion of the Antimasonic majority in the state. This put Pennsylvania out of the proposed convention. Rhode Island had also declined being represented, and Massachusetts had refused to acknowledge delegates from New York and Ohio where the party organization had not been maintained. According to Adams, a convention became merely a meeting of Massachusetts and Vermont to confer upon general matters having no bearing on the presidency. "Thus I hope the idea of a Webster-Van Buren-Antimasonic Convention will fail." The next point was to ascertain if Van Buren was disposed to receive Webster. "If he does, the Antimasons will inevitably be crushed and I must bid goodbye to a troubled sea," Adams concluded. "If he does not, why then Mr. Webster and his friends must stand aloof in our places." Alexander H. Everett, with whom Adams discussed the matter, thought the Antimasons should "*go on*" and keep up a fire upon the Websterites under which they were evidently quailing. He would go to Washington in a few days and see Van Buren. In the meantime, Adams was gratified, looking back over the past few months, to see how "even handed justice has commended the poison prepared for others back to their own lips. A miserable scheme has been most miserably ended."[70]

On December 29, Hallett came to see Adams with letters from two of the Antimasonic seceders, Irwin and Gilleland, who, writing "under the excitement of defeat and mortified pride," urged the Massachusetts Antimasons to give over their hostilities to Webster, who, deserted on all sides, sought shelter with the Antimasons. "Joined with this are projects in plenty ingenious enough but utterly without basis," Adams wrote acidly, "evidently straws at which these drowning men are catching. They have committed a folly and must now set about repenting to which they are ill disposed." Hallett read his reply to Adams, which the latter thought "extremely judicious." The two men again talked over their proposed course, which was not to acknowledge the seceders, to discourage a national convention, but not absolutely to refuse to attend. Still later letters gave a better clue to the plot, "which was a nomination of Webster by this National Convention." At the same time, however, a letter signed "Massachusetts" appeared in the *National Intelligencer*, "evidently by authority," which announced that Webster was not to withdraw as a Whig candidate, and also an editorial in the Boston *Atlas* of December 31 to the same purport. "This sets us more at ease," Adams noted with relief. "There is now no prospect of that union which more than any thing was to be dreaded by us. And hereafter we may in all possibility find plain sailing."[71]

Meanwhile, the Webster cause, reeling from the decision of the Harrisburg convention, immediately received a second shock.

A Maryland Whig Convention met in Baltimore on December 22, 1835, with the Harrison men in complete control. H. M. Stuart wrote to Cushing that "3 fourths of the delegates now assembled, were at the time of their appointments in favor of nominating Mr. Webster and for the life of me I cannot find what has produced the change." Harrison's friends were actively urging his nomination on the grounds of expediency and were using Webster's correspondence with the Pennsylvania Antimasons against him. The "intelligent portion" of the delegates were disposed to adjourn, but Stuart feared a majority would be in favor of making a nomination.[72]

The Webster Whigs moved to adjourn the convention until May 2, but were voted down, and on December 23, the meeting nominated Harrison for President and John Tyler for Vice President. Stuart thought the nomination "a strange result, for 4/5 of those present admit that Mr. Webster is their first choice— they have been frightened into the measure by an array of names which ought never to have been brought to bear on this subject." Harrison's nomination had been urged as the wish and advice of Henry Clay and other prominent men who had heretofore preached against military chieftains. Some of Webster's friends thought the General's nomination might still be successfully resisted, but Stuart doubted it. Still, as long as the Senator remained in the field, his Maryland friends would stick to him and "think it higher honor to *fail* with him, than be successful under the banner of a more fortunate leader."[73]

Webster's friends could do little more than nail his colors to the mast and sink gallantly. The action of the Antimasons and Whigs of Pennsylvania followed by that of the Maryland Whigs effectively scuttled his candidacy. Nathan Sargent wrote Cushing from Philadelphia "that we can [not] do any thing in this state for him."[74] The convention called by the Webster Whigs of Allegheny County, to meet in Harrisburg on January 4, 1836, was indefinitely postponed. "I cannot see that any good can come to you in Pennsylvania by nominating Mr. Webster," Congressman Abbott Lawrence of Massachusetts wrote a Philadelphia Whig at the end of February, "—and you will permit me to say under all circumstances such a course might, and I think would, be productive of mortification and regret to him."[75] As John J. Crittenden, a Clay Whig from Kentucky, remarked, Pennsylvania had decided the contest against Webster, for without that state's support he stood no chance.[76]

## NOTES

*1.* Clay to John Bailhache, September 13, 1835, *Works of Clay,* V, 399-400.

*2.* Barbour to Henry Clay, August 2, 1835, *ibid.,* p. 398.

*3.* Biddle to Herman Cope, August 11, 1835, *Biddle Correspondence,* pp. 255-256.

*4.* Washington *National Intelligencer,* April 2, 1835, quoting Harrisburg *Intelligencer,* January 22, 1835.

*5.* Biddle to Herman Cope, August 11, 1835, *Biddle Correspondence,* pp. 255-256.

*6.* Harrison to William Ayres, May 13, 1835, quoted in Cleaves, *Old Tippecanoe,* p. 296; Harrison to John Tipton, October 9, 1835, in Nellie Armstrong Robertson and Dorothy Riker (eds.), *The John Tipton Papers. Indiana Historical Collections,* vol. XXVI (Indianapolis, 1942), p. 174.

*7.* Samuel B. Findlay to George P. Torrence, September 3, 1835, "Torrence Papers, IV," 82-84.

*8.* Trevor to George P. Torrence, September 12, 1835, *ibid.,* pp. 84-85.

*9.* Niles' *Weekly Register,* XLIX (1835), 155; Washington *National Intelligencer,* October 27, 1835, quoting Harrisburg *Intelligencer,* October 15, 1835.

*10.* Russell J. Ferguson (ed.), "Minutes of the Young Men's Whig Association of Pittsburgh, 1834," *Western Pennsylvania Historical Magazine,* XIX (1936), 213-220.

*11.* Henry R. Mueller, *The Whig Party in Pennsylvania* (New York, 1922), pp. 16-19; J. Cutler Andrews, "The Antimasonic Movement in Western Pennsylvania," *Western Pennsylvania Historical Magazine,* XVIII (1935), 255-266; Charles McCool Snyder, *The Jacksonian Heritage: Pennsylvania Politics, 1833-1848* (Harrisburg, 1958), pp. 50-67.

*12.* Snyder, *Jacksonian Heritage,* pp. 68-69; Stevens to Literary Society of LaFayette College, March 19, 1836, quoted in Richard N. Current, "Love, Hate, and Thaddeus Stevens," *Pennsylvania History,* XIV (1947), 264n.

*13.* Edward Everett to Nathan Sargent, October 26, 1835, Private and Confidential Letterbook of Edward Everett, Massachusetts Historical Society, Boston. (Hereafter cited as Everett Letterbook.)

*14. Register of Debates in Congress,* 23rd Cong., 1st Sess., X, part 2 (Washington, 1834), 1862.

*15.* Everett to Thaddeus Stevens, October 20, 1835, Everett Letterbook.

*16.* Everett to Joseph Ritner, October 20, 1835, *ibid.*

*17.* Quoted in Thomas Frederick Woodley, *Thaddeus Stevens* (Harrisburg, 1934), p. 38.

*18. Ibid.*

*19.* Everett to Thaddeus Stevens, November 2, 1835, Everett Letterbook.

*20.* Stevens to John B. Wallace, October 24, 1835, John William Wallace Collection, Historical Society of Pennsylvania, Philadelphia. (Hereafter cited as Wallace Collection.)

*21.* Everett to Thaddeus Stevens, November 2, 1835, Everett Letterbook.

*22.* Philadelphia *National Gazette,* November 18, 1835; Ralph Korngold, *Thaddeus Stevens: A Being Darkly Wise and Rudely Great* (New York, 1955), p. 26.

*23.* Blakeslee, "Antimasonic Party," II, 319-320; Charles Francis Adams Diary, May 22, 1835; Albany *Argus,* June 23, 1835, quoting Boston *Advocate,* n.d. Harrison's candidacy had not yet assumed serious proportions when Hallett began his campaign on behalf of Van Buren.

*24.* Everett to Harmar Denny, October 20, 1835, Everett Letterbook; Everett to Thaddeus Stevens, November 23, 1835, *ibid.*

*25.* Denny to William Heister, October 19, 1835, quoted in Harmar Denny, "Anti-Masonic Days Recalled," *Lancaster County Historical Society Papers,* XV (1911), 227-229.

*26.* Philadelphia *National Gazette,* November 21, 1835.

*27. Ibid.,* November 16, 1835; Denny to Daniel Webster, November 11, 1835, Webster Papers.

*28.* Harmar Denny *et al.* to Daniel Webster, November 11, 1835, Webster Papers.

*29.* Webster to Harmar Denny *et al.,* November 20, 1835, *Writings and Speeches,* XVIII, 12-14.

*30.* Irwin to Daniel Webster, November 27, 1835, Webster Papers.

*31.* Boston *Courier,* December 16, 1835. Webster's letter offended some Whig Masons and according to a Democratic leader in Massachusetts "has driven many of his own party over to ours" (W. Wright to Amos Kendall, January 7, 1836, Van Buren Papers). To Charles P. Huntington, a Whig leader in Northampton, Webster wrote that he was "exceedingly sorry that any worthy and good men should be hurt by my letter to the Anti-Masons of Pennsylvania. I hope, however, they will do me the justice to believe that I have expressed only my honest and sincere opinions" (February 20, 1836, in Charles P. Huntington, "Diary and Letters of Charles P. Huntington," *Massachusetts Historical Society Proceedings,* LVII [1924], 271).

*32.* Webster to Joseph Wallace *et al.,* November 28, 1835, *Writings and Speeches,* XVI, 259-260.

*33.* Webster to William W. Irwin, November 20, 1835, *ibid.,* pp. 260-261.

*34.* Joseph Wallace and Joseph Shock to William Henry Harrison, April 22, 1835, quoted in Philadelphia *National Gazette,* October 22, 1835; Harrison to Joseph Wallace and Joseph Shock, May 6, 1835, *ibid.*

*35.* Irwin to Daniel Webster, November 27, 1835, Webster Papers.

*36.* Philadelphia *National Gazette,* October 21, 1835, quoting Pittsburgh *Gazette,*

October 17, 1835; Everett to Harmar Denny, October 20, 1835, Everett Letterbook; Everett to Thaddeus Stevens, October 20, 1835, *ibid.*

*37.* Quoted in Cleaves, *Old Tippecanoe,* p. 299.

*38.* Philadelphia *National Gazette,* November 17, 1835, quoting *Pittsburgh Advocate,* November 13, 1835.

*39. Ibid.,* November 13, 1835; Albany *Argus,* November 17, 1835, quoting Boston *Courier,* n.d.; Boston *Courier,* November 14, 1835.

*40.* B. W. Richards to John McLean, January 29, 1835, quoted in Reed, "Emergence of the Whig Party in the North," p. 338.

*41.* Everett to Nathan Sargent, October 26, 1835, Everett Letterbook.

*42.* Everett to Nicholas Biddle, November 3, 1835, Biddle Papers.

*43.* Philadelphia *National Gazette,* November 10, 1835.

*44.* Biddle to Edward Everett, November 12, 1835, President's Letter Book No. 5. B.U.S. When Everett learned the result of the meeting, his fears subsided, and he thought it "under the circumstances of the case . . . not . . . much to be regretted" (Everett to Nicholas Biddle, November 16, 1835, Biddle Papers).

*45. Niles' Weekly Register,* XLIX (1835), 201, quoting Pittsburgh *Advocate,* November 9, 1835; Philadelphia *National Gazette,* November 20, 1835, quoting Wyoming (Penn.) *Herald,* n.d.; Philadelphia *National Gazette,* November 18, 19, 27, 1835.

*46.* Ayres to William Henry Harrison, November 11, 1835, quoted in *Niles' Weekly Register,* XLIX (1835), 244.

*47.* Harrison to William Ayres, November 20, 1835, *ibid.*

*48.* Samuel F. Vinton to William Greene, December 11, 1835, in L. Belle Hamlin (ed.), "Selections from the William Greene Papers, II," *Quarterly Publication of the Historical and Philosophical Society of Ohio,* XIV (1919), 13.

*49.* Boston *Daily Advertiser and Patriot,* December 23, 1835.

*50.* Cushing to Edward Everett, December 17, 1835, Everett Papers.

*51.* Washington *National Intelligencer,* December 2, 1835; Caleb Cushing to Daniel Webster, December 2, 1835, Cushing Papers; Webster to Caleb Cushing, December 6, 1835, quoted in Fuess, *Caleb Cushing,* I, 172-173.

*52.* Tuckerman, *Hone Diary,* I, 177.

*53.* Alexander K. McClure, *Old Time Notes of Pennsylvania* (Philadelphia, 1905), I, 31-32.

*54.* Soloman W. Roberts, "Reminiscences of the First Railroad Over the Allegheny Mountain," *Pennsylvania Magazine of History and Biography,* II (1878), 383.

*55.* Snyder, *Jacksonian Heritage,* p. 70; Mueller, *Whig Party,* p. 30; Washington *National Intelligencer,* December 18, 1835; *Niles' Weekly Register,* XLIX (1835), 287-288, quoting Harrisburg *Intelligencer,* n.d. The seceders were: Thaddeus Stevens, Harmar Denny, Neville Craig, Benjamin Darlington, William W. Irwin, James C. Gilleland, Samuel and Francis Parke, and Charles Ogle.

*56.* Washington *National Intelligencer,* December 18, 1835; Harrisburg *Pennsylvania Reporter and Democratic Herald,* January 5, 1836.

57. Adams, *Memoirs*, IX, 273-274.

58. Rush to Martin Van Buren, January 22, 1836, Van Buren Papers.

59. Mueller, *Whig Party*, pp. 30-31.

60. Van Buren to William W. Irwin *et al.*, May 19, 1836, James C. Gilleland to Martin Van Buren, May 30, 1836, Van Buren Papers; Harrison to the committee of the Antimasonic National Convention, May 29, 1836, quoted in Washington *Globe*, September 5, 1840.

61. Harrison to William Sheets, October 27, 1836, "Letter from William Henry Harrison, 1836," *Virginia Magazine of History and Biography*, XVIII (1910), 109; Goebel, *William Henry Harrison*, p. 314.

62. Washington *National Intelligencer*, December 21, 1835; Boston *Courier*, December 24, 1835.

63. Albany *Argus*, January 5, 1836, quoting Philadelphia *National Gazette*, n.d.

64. Mueller, *Whig Party*, p. 30n.

65. Nathan Sargent to Caleb Cushing, December 29, 1835, Cushing Papers.

66. Miner to Daniel Webster, December 17, 1835, Webster Papers. In his disgust with the Harrison men, Miner suggested that the friends of Webster take up White, with Horace Binney, Samuel L. Southard, John Davis, Edward Everett, or some other Whig on the ticket for vice-president, which would insure the judge's election by the Electoral College. Miner thought that if the North yielded the presidency to the South for one term, "could we not claim it for a Northern man the next; and might not that man be Mr. Webster? Would not the election of Mr. V.B. shut out all hope of Mr. W. for sure?" (Miner to John B. Wallace, January 13, 1836, Wallace Collection).

67. Harrisburg *Pennsylvania Reporter and Democratic Herald*, January 5, 1836.

68. Charles Francis Adams Diary, December 17, 18, 21, 22, 1835.

69. *Ibid.*, December 26, 1835.

70. *Ibid.*, December 26, 28, 1835.

71. *Ibid.*, December 29, 31, 1835.

72. Stuart to Caleb Cushing, December 22, 1835, Cushing Papers.

73. *Niles' Weekly Register*, XLIX (1835), 288; Stuart to Caleb Cushing, December 23, 1835, Cushing Papers.

74. Sargent to Caleb Cushing, December 29, 1835, Cushing Papers.

75. Lawrence to John B. Wallace, February 29, 1836, Wallace Collection.

76. Crittenden to James T. Morehead *et al.*, December 23, 1835, quoted in Goebel, *William Henry Harrison*, p. 315.

# EPILOGUE

8 The question now arose as to what course Webster and his friends would pursue, and the correspondent of the Boston *Daily Advertiser* in Washington reported much "solicitude" among Whig leaders on this subject. Wrote Senator John J. Crittenden: "Webster's pretensions are considered virtually at an end, but, as yet, he says nothing, and, as far as I can hear, his course is not ascertained. He deserves the kindest and most repectful treatment from the public on this occasion, that he may fall like a great man."[1] The New York Whigs, William H. Seward declared later, wanted Webster to withdraw in favor of Harrison; and Henry Clay also urged his retirement.[2] But his closest friends were determined to uphold his candidacy, even though they admitted privately that he had no chance in 1836.[3] Caleb Cushing wrote a letter signed "MASSACHUSETTS," which was published in the *National Intelligencer* on December 28, 1835, in which he denounced the selection of Harrison by the Whigs and Antimasons and indicated what course the Webster men intended to pursue. It said:

The conflict before us, nay the conflict upon us, is a contest for the preservation of the Constitution. This, at least, is the profound conviction of the people of Massachusetts. . . . Animated by this feeling, they will support Mr. Webster. Whoever may be seduced or whoever terrified, whoever may follow or whoever fly, . . . *they* still rally to the banner of the Constitution as upborne by him, with the most entire and absolute confidence. . . .4

Still, rumors drifted back to Massachusetts that Webster was ready to withdraw. Amos A. Lawrence, who was visiting his uncle, Abbott Lawrence, in Washington, reported that the senior Lawrence was having great difficulty in holding the Massachusetts delegation firmly behind Webster, since "each is looking for his own candidate—*beyond* Mr. Webster," and "it requires infinite resource to make them hang together, and I think that before this there would have been a scattering unless he had held them together." "Mr. Webster looks very gloomy since the Harrisburg convention," he added, "and hesitates about doing what the Massachusetts delegation wait for. When he does withdraw I think there will be some commotion among them."5 Abbott Lawrence himself admitted that "upon the whole we feel ourselves placed in an awkward position—*Our stock appears to be used up and we have no means of replacing it of a quality that suits our taste or judgement.*"6

It was also rumored that Everett was preparing to abandon Webster, but this the Governor vigorously denied. He assured Cushing that he had uniformly advised adhering to Webster to the last, even if Massachusetts, in so doing, should stand alone— "which, however, I have never predicted she would." He had written a letter approving the sentiments of "MASSACHUSETTS," and had asked John O. Sargent to copy it into the *Atlas,* and Hale had published it in the *Advertiser.* He concluded fervently:

I hope among all the other things which Mr. W. has to disgust him, he will not think he has any cause of complaint against me. His continuance as a candidate here is identical with my own, in my humble sphere; & were it not, I had rather sink with him than rise without him;—& this he cannot doubt.7

Most Whig leaders in Massachusetts considered Webster's remaining in the race as essential to the preservation of the Whig hegemony in the state. His withdrawal, it was predicted, would throw the party organization into confusion at the very time that its control was being strongly challenged by the Democratic party. Robert C. Winthrop, while recognizing that the Massachusetts Whigs would have to fight "a lost battle," wrote that "so long as we can save Massachusetts, we have something left; and this we cannot do under any name but Webster's. So say the best judges in the Legislature & the best fellows everywhere, and so I believe."[8] Noting the efforts of Harrison's agents to secure Webster's retirement as an aid to the General's campaign in Ohio, New York, and Pennsylvania, Caleb Cushing stated the situation succinctly: "Considering the subject in a national point of view, the question is this: is it our duty, by the withdrawal of Mr. Webster, to sacrifice the Whig cause & the State Administration in Massachusetts, in order by possibility to aid the Whig cause in Ohio? I say, no."[9]

Webster wished to withdraw from the canvass, but he deferred to party leaders in Massachusetts and remained in the field.[10] At the end of February, as a formality, he addressed a letter to H. W. Kinsman in Boston, to be read before the Whig members of the legislature stating his own personal wish to withdraw. He had been restrained from doing so "only by the consideration that there are interests, which might be affected by such a movement, in regard to which the opinions of others ought to be consulted." He would therefore leave the question of withdrawal to friends in Massachusetts and "cheerfully abide" by their decision.[11]

On March 10 the Whig legislators met in Boston, reaffirmed their nomination of Webster, and selected Francis Granger for Vice-President. The meeting then adjourned until March 24. In the meantime, an invitation was published in the newspapers inviting those Massachusetts towns, not represented by Whig members in the legislature, to send delegates to the adjourned meeting. At the second meeting, Webster's letter to Kinsman was read, after which the delegates unanimously reaffirmed his nomination along with Granger's. Edward Everett was then renominated for governor and George Hull for lieutenant governor.

Finally, the meeting voted to defer the selection of a presidential electoral ticket until the fall.[12]

Meanwhile, the majority of the state's Antimasons had followed Benjamin Hallett into the Democratic party. The two leading objections which party leaders repeatedly urged against Webster were, first, that to vote for him would be useless, since he could not possibly be elected; secondly, that he and his friends opposed John Quincy Adams. On January 29, 1836, an Antimasonic state convention met in Boston and nominated Van Buren for President and Richard M. Johnson for Vice-President.[13]

A minority of the Massachusetts Antimasons continued to support Webster's candidacy. On March 9 this group met in Boston and adopted resolutions recommending him to the state's Antimasons, "well assured that his preeminent qualifications as a Statesman, his attachment to the Constitution, [and] his free and open declaration on the subject of Freemasonry, will place him above all other competitors for the Executive chair, in the estimation of those who desire the Supremacy of the Laws. . . ." For Vice-President, "that firm patriot and consistent Antimason," Francis Granger, was endorsed. The resolutions expressed "disapprobation" of Van Buren's nomination by the Antimasonic state convention as representing a virtual surrender of Antimasonic principles.[14]

The Webster Antimasons issued an "Address to the Antimasonic Republicans of the Commonwealth of Massachusetts" in which they declared that true Antimasons had always opposed Jackson, "a *worthy* brother [Mason], who acknowledges the 'jurisdiction' of the lodge room"; that Hallett's *Advocate* no longer represented true Antimasonry; and that since Van Buren had not openly declared his opposition to Masonry, it would be a desertion of party principles to support his candidacy. Moreover, said the address, Richard M. Johnson was an "adhering Freemason." Webster, on the other hand, had openly stated his sentiments on Masonry "with a frankness that does honor to his heart." He and Granger should be supported with zeal by the Antimasons of Massachusetts in the coming election.[15]

In neighboring Vermont, an Antimasonic state convention

nominated S. H. Jenison for governor and Harrison and Granger
for President and Vice-President. The vote for President was
as follows: Harrison 87, Webster 28, Van Buren 27, Granger 20,
and Edward Everett 1. So Harrison had a majority of the 163
votes cast. On the ballot for Vice-President, the majority was
overwhelmingly for Granger. A Whig convention was in session
at the same time and unanimously ratified these nominations.[16]

It was a rather depressing winter for Webster personally.
Mrs. Webster did not accompany him to Washington for the congressional session, and he went to no evening parties and few
dinners. "I like very much the pleasure of staying at home, &
sitting by the fire, thro' an evening, & never find it dull, tho' I
am alone," he wrote his wife. In late January he gave a dinner
for the Massachusetts delegation, which John Quincy Adams
did not attend. In February he contracted a severe cold which
kept him from attending the Senate except in fair weather. Jackson's nomination of Roger B. Taney as Chief Justice of the
Supreme Court to succeed Marshall deepened his gloom. "Judge
Story arrived last evening, in good health, but bad spirits," he
informed his wife on January 10. "He thinks the Supreme Court
is *gone*, & I think so too; and almost everything else is gone, or
seems rapidly going."[17]

On March 18 Webster was granted a ten day leave of absence,
but did not return to the Senate until April 13. On his arrival in
Boston, he found his wife recovering from a severe attack of
pleurisy. He returned reluctantly to the Capital, and admitted to
John Davis that he had more than half a mind not to return at all.

> I see no good to be done, & there is little, either in or out of
> Congress, to encourage efforts. Our people here maintain tolerably
> good spirits, & will not neglect the fall elections, since the State
> Government depends thereon. But for that consideration, the
> indifference of some, & the disgust of others, would make the
> state a ready sacrifice to the Spoils party. There was a meet'g on
> Monday eve [April 4] at Concert Hall of the Whig members of
> the Legislature, & some other Gentlemen. . . . The Governor
> [Everett] was present, & told some truths, in a very plain manner.
> He said we had nothing to hope, now or at any other time, either

from the South or West, in his opinion. The general feel'g seemed to be that Massachusetts must stand alone, if she stands at all.[18]

Webster's presidential campaign had collapsed completely outside his own state. He did not, as most historians state, "run in New England." The anti-Van Buren men in the North endorsed Harrison-Granger electoral tickets, except in Massachusetts and in Illinois where Harrison shared a combined ticket with White. New York, New Jersey, Ohio, and Indiana held state conventions to second the Pennsylvania nominations. In the South, Kentucky and Delaware Whigs supported Harrison and Granger, Maryland Whigs Harrison and John Tyler. In Virginia and Missouri, a common set of electors served for both Harrison and White; if the Whigs won, electoral votes would go to the man favored by voter write-ins. Elsewhere, White and Tyler slates were drawn up. Only in South Carolina did the legislature still choose the state's electors.[19]

The campaign itself scarcely rose above a personal level. The rivalry of Webster, McLean, Clay, and Harrison dampened the enthusiasm with which the Whigs had begun the contest. Jeremiah Mason predicted that since Webster had withdrawn except in Massachusetts, "the Whigs of New England will make no effort to sustain Harrison or White."[20] In the spring elections in Connecticut and Rhode Island, the Democrats swept the governorships and state legislatures. Party journals tried to revive lagging spirits by parading the tired steed of "executive usurpation" before the people. The Tennessee frontiersman and former congressman, Colonel Davy Crockett, lent his name to a scurrilous *Life of Martin Van Buren,* written by Augustin S. Clayton of Georgia in the interests of the White campaign.[21] In one respect the Whig party profited by the lesson of 1832; it made no serious attempt to bring the Bank issue into the election.

Probably few Whigs expected success. As early as the spring of 1835 William H. Seward explained to his friend, Thurlow Weed, why Van Buren would win. "The people are for him. Not so much for him as for the principle they suppose he represents. That principle is Democracy," he wrote. "It is with them, the poor against the rich; and it is not to be disguised that, since the last election, the array of parties has very strongly taken that character. Those who felt themselves or believed themselves poor have fallen off very naturally from us, and into the majority, whose success proved them to be the friends of the poor; while the rich *we* 'have always with us.' " He added that the Whig papers had maneuvered themselves unconsciously into the politically indefensible position of apologizing for the rich.[22]

John Quincy Adams was so pessimistic as Seward. Henry Clay and John C. Calhoun "are left upon the field for dead"; he told his diary, "and men of straw, Hugh L. White, William H. Harrison, and Daniel Webster, are thrust forward in their places." None of them had a principle to lean upon, while Van Buren's principle was the "talisman of democracy, which, so long as this Union lasts, can never fail." Returning to Washington from Boston in November 1836, Adams found the excitement of a presidential election all along the road. "White and Harrison are now the golden calves of the people," he wrote sardonically, "and their dull sayings are repeated for wit, and their grave inanity is passed off for wisdom." Being an Adams, he attributed this election ardor to the practice of betting on the outcome, which added a spur of private, personal, and pecuniary interest to the impulse of patriotism.[23]

Massachusetts Whigs held a state convention in Worcester on September 14, 1836, to select an electoral ticket for President and Vice-President. In an address to the voters of the state, the convention noted the probability that the election would go into the House of Representatives, and promised that, when the proper time arrived, the Massachusetts delegation would act "for the country and the whole country." In the meantime, the Massachusetts Whigs must see that the state's electoral vote did not go to Van Buren and Johnson, and this could be best accomplished by continuing to support Webster's candidacy. Said the Convention: "We know of no other way, so far as on us depends, to defeat the nominations of the Baltimore Convention, but to go straight forward . . . in the course that has been . . . adopted and repeatedly approved."[24] The Whig press in Massachusetts generally ignored the national election, believing the

state to be safe for Webster, and devoted their columns to an
unrestrained abuse of all the Democratic candidates in the state,
including Alexander H. Everett, who was running for election
from the ninth (Norfolk) district, and George Bancroft in the
seventh.[25]

The fall election in Massachusetts brought victory for both
Webster and the state ticket although, as John Quincy Adams
noted, "The returns are marked by some extraordinary peculiari-
ties."[26] The Whigs were significantly weaker than in 1835. The
increase in the total vote for governor was more than 13,000
votes; however, Everett's majority over Marcus Morton was only
6,168 votes (42,160 to 35,992). Morton's vote rose 10,765, while
Everett gained only 4,605. The accession of Antimasons and
Workingmen to the Democratic party made up a sizable portion
of Morton's increase. In the presidential contest Webster and
Granger received 42,247 votes to 35,474 for Van Buren and
Johnson. Webster carried nine counties and Van Buren five. On
the other hand, Van Buren polled a higher percentage of the two-
party vote in the state than any Democratic candidate until 1852.
He received approximately twenty-one thousand more votes than
Jackson had won in 1832.[27] After the election a disappointed
Hone wrote, "The very thought (wild and hopeless as it is)
of having Daniel Webster President of the United States should
make the heart of every American leap in his bosom and cause
him to dream of the days of George Washington."[28]

Webster gave his electors permission to cast their ballots "in
the manner they think most likely to be useful in supporting the
constitution and laws of the country, the union of the States, the
perpetuity of our republican institutions, and the important
interests of the whole country; and in maintaining the character
of Massachusetts for integrity, honor, national patriotism, and
fidelity to the constitution."[29] The New York *Commercial Advertiser* was undoubtedly correct when it reported that Webster
wanted his electors to vote for Harrison if the result of the election
seemed to favor his candidacy.[30]

Van Buren, however, gained a clear but by no means overwhelming victory. White carried Georgia and Tennessee; the

Massachusetts electors gave their 14 votes to Webster; Harrison won in Ohio, Indiana, Kentucky, Maryland, Delaware, New Jersey, and Vermont; and elsewhere north of the Potomac, except in New York, ran close on Van Buren's heels. The South Carolina legislature at first resolved almost unanimously against voting for any one of the presidential candidates, but doubts arose whether a state could vote blank, and the name of Senator Willie P. Mangum of North Carolina was inserted. Van Buren had the rest, with 170 electoral votes to 124 for the opposition. Because the Virginia Democracy would not support Richard M. Johnson for the vice-presidency he received just half the total votes (147); and the election, for the first and only time in history, went to the Senate, which chose the Kentuckian.

The Democrats had little cause for rejoicing. The national vote gave Van Buren a majority of only 25,688 out of 1,505,290 votes cast. The Democratic ticket won 557 counties in the nation, while the several Whig candidates carried 485.[31] For the first time in our political history, a fairly evenly balanced two-party system had emerged in nearly every state in the union. The Whig strategy of throwing the election into the House had come very close to success. A shift of approximately 2,100 votes in Pennsylvania from Van Buren to Harrison would have given the state to the Ohioan and denied Van Buren an electoral majority. Once the election was in the House, a sufficient number of southern Jacksonians might have defected to give the presidency to White or Harrison.

In the election of 1836 the two party system was for the first time extended to the South and West.[32] It may be said that in 1832 there was no National Republican party in the lower South, and in the upper South, only in Delaware, Maryland, and Kentucky. Clay's total vote in the slaveholding states was less than 87,000 with Jackson about 100,000 votes ahead of him in the same area. Since the General had no organized opposition in Georgia, Alabama, Mississippi, and Louisiana, he polled a small vote in those states in 1832. In South Carolina the legislature voted for Governor John Floyd of Virginia. This kind of one-party politics typical of the South came to an abrupt end between 1834 and 1836 and by election time a balanced two-party system had emerged. Van Buren's candidacy was a crucial stimulus to this development. There was a vague but persistent suspicion of the New Yorker among some southern Jacksonians, a feeling "that Mr. Van Buren has always had a leaning towards putting the negroes on the same footing with the whites," as the Washington *United States Telegraph* charged;[33] and those politicians who were disposed to challenge the "regular" Jacksonian leadership in any state, the so-called "Collar Men," but feared to break with Jackson, could denounce Van Buren with impunity. The nomination of Hugh Lawson White gave these men an alternative candidate from their own region. In Tennessee White scored a greater victory, both in percentage of the vote and number of counties carried, than any other Whig was able to do later, even in the banner Whig years of 1840 and 1848. In 1836 Van Buren polled slightly less than fifty per cent of the popular vote in the slaveholding states (excluding South Carolina), and it is remarkable that he lost only two of the normally Democratic states in this area, Georgia and Tennessee, although his majorities were small in Mississippi and Louisiana. Undoubtedly, he profited in the South from a widespread belief that the sole object of the White campaign was to throw the election into the House in order that Harrison might be made President—in other words, that Judge White was a mere "stalking-horse" to effect this result.

In the Old Northwest, Ohio and Indiana fell into the Whig column, while in Illinois and Michigan, Van Buren's majorities were slight. The marked *shifting* of votes to the Whig party in the northwestern states came in 1836 not in the famous log-cabin hard-cider campaign of 1840.[34] In 1832 Clay had polled 48.5 per cent of the vote in Ohio; Harrison won his own state with a percentage of 52.1. In Indiana the shift was even greater, for while Clay had polled a mere 32.1 per cent, Harrison gained 55.9 per cent of the vote.[35] A historian of the region has concluded that "the support of the church people of the Northwest, which had never been given to Clay, was thrown to Harrison."[36] Party lines were still fluid in the West. Many of the same men who had voted for the "Hero of New Orleans" in 1824, 1828, and

1832, rejoiced in 1836 to give their ballot for the hero of Tippe-canoe and the War of 1812 in the Northwest. Clay, however, they would not support. In 1839 Senator Oliver H. Smith of Indiana told the Kentuckian: "No name under heaven would be so well calculated as yours, to stimulate your original supporters of our party to a desperate contest. But on that class who joined us under the Harrison flag we can not rely, should you be the candidate. They have not forgotten the old contest when their idol General Jackson and yourself were in the field."[37]

Harrison's strong showing in 1836 surprised the professionals and went a long way toward determining the action of the Whig national convention at Harrisburg in December 1839. During the campaign, Seward had written Weed: "I do, every day and every hour, see evidence that General Harrison is capable of being made, under any other circumstances than the present, an invincible candidate. But the time has not come; the great issue is pressed upon us before men are ripe." After the election, Seward, looking toward 1840, hailed the "hero of Tippecanoe" as "a candidate by continuation."[38] According to the famous New York editor, Horace Greeley, when the election returns came "pouring in" to New York, there was a "general waking up to the conviction that either Harrison was more popular, or Van Buren more obnoxious than had been supposed in our State, and that the latter might have been beaten by seasonable concert and effort."[39] The Whigs took heart from a general belief that Van Buren was vulnerable. Calhoun wrote James Hammond that the election had ended, as was anticipated, with a Democratic victory; but one far less decisive than was expected by friend or foe. "It is quite certain, that the President elect did not receive a majority of votes, and that, if the opposition had known their strength, he could have been defeated easily. The general impression is that he cannot maintain himself. The opposition shows no indication of yielding, while his own party is agitated by conflicts within."[40] As Horace Greeley later perceived, "In that slouching Whig defeat of 1836 lay the germ of the overwhelming Whig triumph of 1840."[41]

Such reflections were no consolation to Webster, who, as

the months passed, still grieved at his defeat. During a visit to Exeter in August 1836, he privately "expressed himself in the most despondent terms; said he was tired of life, and did not care what became of him. . . ." In September William Plumer found that he was depressed and gloomy in his feelings, "felt sore at his own ill success in the canvass," and attributed some part of his apparent unpopularity to Clay. Plumer gave a striking characterization of Webster's driving impulses:

> Webster is ambitious; and can be satisfied with nothing short of the highest. He has acquired all the fame which mere speechmaking can confer on him, but he has no substantial power adequate to his desires or the acknowledged force of his mind. He has long served under men whom he does not like and whom he considers his inferiors in mental power. His attempt to form a party of his own . . . has been unsuccessful and he feels that Clay though his inferior in many respects is yet the acknowledged leader of the Whig party.[42]

Webster rationalized his defeat by blaming Clay and the western Whigs, and the passage of years did not lessen his conviction that they had betrayed him in 1836 by giving their support to Harrison. As he wrote to Governor Robert P. Letcher, a Clay man, in 1843:

> I will be frank. I think . . . that a certain party, or division of the Whigs, mostly in the West and South, have not extended, in times past, that cordial respect towards some of us . . . which they have received from us. For instance, in 1836, there was no Kentucky candidate before the people; there was a Massachusetts candidate. How did Kentucky act? And, let me add, it was Kentucky in the course adopted by her in 1836, that gave a new and unexpected direction to Whig preferences and kept her own favorite son from the place in which she wishes to see him. I need not prove this; reflect upon it, and you will find it is just so. But let that pass. We all finally concurred in General Harrison's election.[43]

Webster, despite some character flaws, was a man of exceptional ability; he would have been an abler President than many of those who occupied the White House between Jackson and Lincoln. But since 1828 the presidency has usually been awarded

on grounds other than fitness: to the best candidate but not necessarily to the best man. The most effective way to attract the
average voter, politicians soon discovered, was to flatter him. The
managers who took up Jackson because he was popular with the
people first organized this new system. In the election of 1836
the Whigs imitated their opponents by adopting the politics of
availability. At no time were Webster's chances for the presidency
good; after his party made expediency rather than talents or
principles the criteria for selection, the "God-like's" prospects
dwindled to the vanishing point. Unfortunately for Webster's
peace of mind, he never could realize this, and the recurring
fourth-year frustration of his ambition left him disappointed and
embittered. To the last he clung to the delusion that only a
"great body of implacable enemies" had kept him from the
presidency.[44]

## NOTES

*1.* Boston *Daily Advertiser and Patriot,* January 1, 1836; Crittenden to Orlando
Brown, December 27, 1835, quoted in Mrs. Chapman Coleman (ed.), *The Life of
John J. Crittenden, With Selections from His Correspondence and Speeches*
(Philadelphia, 1871), I, 88-89. Crittenden also reported that "Harrison's friends
here dread nothing more than that White should be scared off the field, or his
friends discouraged from giving him a zealous support, and perhaps relapsing into
Van Burenism. To avoid this is a point of obvious policy and I think it is neither
right nor politic to exaggerate Harrison's prospects at the expense of White's. . . .
At this moment of some alarm with him and his friends, it is better to increase
than diminish their hopes."

*2.* Seward, *Autobiography,* pp. 298-299; Clay to Hugh Lawson White, August 27,
1838, quoted in Nancy N. Scott (ed.), *A Memoir of Hugh Lawson White, Judge of
the Supreme Court of Tennessee, Member of the Senate of the United States, etc.
With Selections from His Speeches and Correspondence* (Philadelphia, 1856),
p. 367.

*3.* Caleb Cushing to Edward Everett, December 24, 1835, Everett Papers; Edward Everett to Caleb Cushing, December 23, 28, 1835, Cushing Papers.

*4.* Washington *National Intelligencer,* December 28, 1835. "You may see in the
papers an article from the Intelligencer signed Massachusetts," Cushing wrote to
his father. "The Harrison men are crying out against it as Van Burenism. Do
not believe them. . . . I wrote the piece on reflection, & in consultation with the
*most responsible members* of our Delegation; & I am persuaded it indicates the
only course that Massachusetts can safely and honorably pursue" (Cushing to
J. W. Cushing, December 30, 1835, Cushing Papers).

5. Amos Adams Lawrence to his father, January 8, 1836, "Letters of Amos Adams Lawrence," *Massachusetts Historical Society Proceedings*, LIII (1919), 52-53.

6. Lawrence to John B. Wallace, February 29, 1836, Wallace Collection.

7. Everett to Caleb Cushing, January 4, 1836, quoted in Fuess, *Caleb Cushing*, I, 174.

8. Theophilus Parsons to Caleb Cushing, February 22, 1836, *ibid.*, p. 200; Winthrop to Caleb Cushing, February 25, 1836, *ibid.*, pp. 200-201.

9. Cushing to Theophilus Parsons, undated, *ibid.*, p. 200. The Boston *Courier* declared that the Whigs of Massachusetts would vote for Webster, "leaving the question of *availability* to be settled, as it always has been and always will be, by office-seekers, demagogues and political mendicants" (February 18, 1836).

10. Webster to J. Watson Webb, May 6, 1836, *Writings and Speeches*, XVI, 277.

11. Webster to H. W. Kinsman, February 27, 1836, quoted in Washington *National Intelligencer*, March 31, 1836.

12. Boston *Advertiser*, March 17, 26, 28, 1836; Boston *Courier*, March 14, 28, 1836.

13. Blakeslee, "Antimasonic Party," II, 323; Darling, *Political Changes in Massachusetts*, p. 194.

14. *Resolutions Adopted by the Antimasonic Members of the Legislature of Massachusetts, and Other Citizens of Boston and the Vicinity, Opposed to the Nomination of Martin Van Buren and Richard M. Johnson for President and Vice President of the U. S. At a Meeting Held in the Chamber of the House of Representatives, March 9, 1836. With an Address to Their Antimasonic Fellow Citizens Throughout the State* (Boston, 1836), pp. 3-4.

15. *Ibid.*, pp. 5-24. In rebuttal Hallett charged that the Webster Antimasonic Convention had contained only fifteen persons who had even been Antimasons. But Arthur Darling concludes, in spite of Hallett's assertions, that "its officers and prominent members had good claims to be Antimasons" (Darling, *Political Changes in Massachusetts*, p. 194).

16. *Niles' Weekly Register*, L (1836), 33.

17. Webster to Mrs. Caroline Webster, January 10, 24, February 9, 1836, *Letters of Webster*, pp. 198, 200, 203.

18. Webster to John Davis, April 7, 1836, *Writings and Speeches*, XVI, 274.

19. Washington *National Intelligencer*, December 24, 28, 1835; *Niles' Weekly Register*, L (1836), 1, 266. The New Jersey Whig State Convention, after nominating Harrison and Granger, resolved "that we entertain the highest opinion of the eminent abilities and patriotism of the Hon. Daniel Webster" (John Scott to Daniel Webster, June 6, 1836, Webster Papers).

20. Mason to George Ticknor, April 3, 1836, quoted in Clark, *Memoir of Jeremiah Mason*, p. 351.

21. J. D. Wade, "The Authorship of David Crockett's 'Autobiography,'" *Georgia Historical Quarterly*, VI (1922), 265-268.

22. Seward to Thurlow Weed, April 12, 1835, quoted in Seward, *Autobiography*, pp. 257-258.

*23.* Adams, *Memoirs*, IX, 276-277, 311-312.

*24.* Boston *Advertiser*, August 1, 1836; Boston *Courier*, September 22, 1836.

*25.* Carroll, *Whig Party*, p. 144; Darling, *Political Changes in Massachusetts*, p. 109.

*26.* Adams, *Memoirs*, IX, 313.

*27.* Darling, *Political Changes in Massachusetts*, p. 200; Walter Dean Burnham, *Presidential Ballots, 1836-1892* (Baltimore, 1955), pp. 18, 510-512.

*28.* Tuckerman, *Hone Diary*, I, 237.

*29.* Webster to Nathaniel Silsbee, November 15, 1835, *Writings and Speeches*, XVIII, 22.

*30.* *Niles' Weekly Register*, LI (1836), 242-243, quoting New York *Commercial Advertiser*, n.d. The Whig electors assembled in the State House in Boston on December 6, 1836, and organized with Nathaniel Silsbee of Salem as President. The next day they met again and voted unanimously for Webster and Granger. General Thomas Langley of Hawley was appointed to carry the official tally of votes to Washington. Nathaniel Silsbee, "Biographical Notes," Essex Institute *Historical Collections*, XXV (1899), 74-75; Boston *Advertiser*, December 8, 1836.

*31.* Burnham, *Presidential Ballots*, p. 17.

*32.* See Richard P. McCormick, *The Second American Party System: Party Formation in the Jacksonian Era* (Chapel Hill, 1966).

*33.* Washington *United States Telegraph*, September 12, 1835.

*34.* Lynch, *Fifty Years of Party Warfare*, p. 472.

*35.* Burnham, *Presidential Ballots*, p. 18.

*36.* R. Carlyle Buley, *The Old Northwest: Pioneer Period, 1815-1840* (Indianapolis, 1950), II, 211.

*37.* Smith to Henry Clay, September 28, 1839, quoted in Smith, *Early Indiana Sketches*, p. 252.

*38.* Seward to Thurlow Weed, February 27, November 17, 1836, quoted in Seward, *Autobiography*, pp. 299, 319.

*39.* Horace Greeley, *Recollections of a Busy Life* (New York, 1868), p. 113.

*40.* Calhoun to James H. Hammond, February 18, 1837, "Calhoun Correspondence," 367.

*41.* Greeley, *Recollections*, p. 113.

*42.* Plumer, "Reminiscences of Daniel Webster," *Writings and Speeches*, XVII, 559-560.

*43.* Webster to Robert P. Letcher, October 23, 1843, *ibid.*, XVI, 414.

*44.* Webster to H. M. Grinnell and others, October 12, 1852, *ibid.*, XVI, 666-667. In one of his last conversations on politics, Webster predicted the defeat of General Winfield Scott, the Whig nominee in 1852, and the dissolution of the Whig Party. The party, he explained, had begun its "downward course" when it abandoned principle for expediency, when "new leaders got in, who wanted office," and nominated available men like Harrison, Zachary Taylor, and now Scott, without regard for high qualifications. See Peter Harvey, *Reminiscences and Anecdotes of Daniel Webster* (Boston, 1877), pp. 198-199.

# BIBLIOGRAPHY

## I. PRIMARY SOURCES

### A. MANUSCRIPTS

Charles Francis Adams Diary and Letterbooks, 1833-1836. Adams Papers, Massachusetts Historical Society, Boston.

Nicholas Biddle Papers, 1794-1843. 113 vols; 6 letter books. This monumental collection contains many letters which are not printed in Professor McGrane's edition of the Biddle correspondence. Manuscript Division, Library of Congress.

Caleb Cushing Papers, 1817-1879. 423 mss boxes, 104 letter file boxes, 33 loose vols., 10 loose pamphlets, 3 loose noteboxes. A valuable collection for this study. Manuscript Division, Library of Congress.

Edward Everett Papers, 1675-1865. 20 mss boxes, 240 bound vols. of letter books and diaries, and a collection of pamphlets in bound vols. Everett's correspondence reveals the Webster Whigs' preoccupation with Pennsylvania politics in 1835. Massachusetts Historical Society, Boston.

Martin Van Buren Papers, 1703-1862. Correspondence, state papers, and notes. Of some value for this study. Manuscript Division, Library of Congress.

John William Wallace Collection, 1725-1854. 1,700 items. Several important letters on Webster's candidacy in Pennsylvania. Historical Society of Pennsylvania, Philadelphia.

Daniel Webster Papers, 1800-1874. 13 vols., 1 scrapbook, 4 boxes. Contains many letters which have not been published in the

various editions of Webster's works.  Manuscript Division, Library
of Congress.

## B. GOVERNMENT DOCUMENTS

*Congressional Globe,* 23rd Cong., 1st & 2nd Sess., 1833-1835.
*Register of Debates in the Congress of the United States,* Twenty-first
  through the Twenty-fourth Congresses, 1829-1835.
Richardson, James D., *A Compilation of the Messages and Papers of
  the Presidents, 1789-1897,* 10 vols.  Washington: Government
  Printing Office, 1896-1899.

## C. NEWSPAPERS AND PERIODICALS

Albany *Argus,* 1833-1835.
Boston *Courier,* 1833-1836.
Boston *Daily Advertiser and Patriot,* 1835-1836.
Boston *Daily Atlas,* 1834-1835.
Concord *New Hampshire Patriot,* 1833.
Harrisburg *Pennsylvania Reporter and Democratic Herald,* 1836.
*New-York American,* 1834-1835.
*Niles' Weekly Register,* 1830-1836.
Philadelphia *National Gazette,* 1833-1835.
Washington *Examiner,* 1833.
Washington *Globe,* 1833-1835.
Washington *National Intelligencer,* 1833-1835.
Washington *United States Telegraph,* 1833-1835.

## D. PAMPHLETS

*Resolutions Adopted by the Antimasonic Members of the Legislature
  of Massachusetts, and Other Citizens of Boston and the Vicinity,
  Opposed to the Nomination of Martin Van Buren and Richard
  M. Johnson for President and Vice President of the U. S. at a
  Meeting Held in the Chamber of the House of Representatives,
  March 9, 1836. With an Address to Their Antimasonic Fellow
  Citizens Throughout the State.* Boston: D. Hooton, Printer, 1836.
Webster, Daniel, *Address to the Citizens of Pittsburgh, July 9, 1833.*
  Boston: Buckingham, 1833.

# E. PUBLISHED CORRESPONDENCE

Bassett, John Spencer (ed.), *The Correspondence of Andrew Jackson,* 6 vols. Washington: Carnegie Institute of Washington, 1926-1933.

Choate, Rufus, "Rufus Choate Letters," Essex Institute *Historical Collections,* LXIX (1933), 81-87.

Colton, Calvin (ed.), *The Private Correspondence of Henry Clay.* New York: A. S. Barnes and Company, 1855.

————, *The Works of Henry Clay,* Federal Edition, 10 vols. New York: G. P. Putnam's Sons, 1904.

Cox, Issac Joslin (ed.), "Selections from the Torrence Papers, I," *Quarterly Publication of the Historical and Philosophical Society of Ohio,* I (1906), 65-96.

————, "Selections from the Torrence Papers, IV," *Quarterly Publication of the Historical and Philosophical Society of Ohio,* III (1908), 66-102.

Gordon, William F. *et al.,* "Original Letters," *William and Mary College Quarterly Historical Magazine,* XXI (1912), 1-11.

Hamilton, Joseph Gregoire de Roulhac (ed.), *The Papers of William Alexander Graham,* 4 vols. Raleigh: State Department of Archives and History, 1957-1961.

Hamlin, L. Belle (ed.), "Selections from the Follett Papers, I," *Quarterly Publication of the Historical and Philosophical Society of Ohio,* V (1910), 34-76.

————, "Selections from the Follett Papers, IV," *Quarterly Publication of the Historical and Philosophical Society of Ohio,* XI (1916), 5-26.

————, "Selections from the William Greene Papers, II," *Quarterly Publication of the Historical and Philosophical Society of Ohio,* XIV (1919), 5-26.

Harrison, William Henry, "Letter from William Henry Harrison, 1836," *Virginia Magazine of History and Biography,* XVIII (1910), 109.

Huntington, Charles P., "Diary and Letters of Charles P. Huntington," *Massachusetts Historical Society Proceedings,* LVII (1924), 244-277.

Jameson, J. Franklin (ed.), "Correspondence of John C. Calhoun," *Annual Report of the American Historical Association,* II (1900).

Lawrence, Amos Adams, "Letters of Amos Adams Lawrence," *Massachusetts Historical Society Proceedings,* LIII (1919), 48-57.

McGrane, Reginald (ed.), *The Correspondence of Nicholas Biddle Dealing with National Affairs, 1807-1844.* Boston: Houghton Mifflin Company, 1919.

McIntyre, James W. (ed.), *The Writings and Speeches of Daniel Webster*, National Edition, 18 vols. Boston: Little, Brown and Company, 1903.

Robertson, Nellie Armstrong and Dorothy Riker (eds.), *The John Tipton Papers*, 3 vols. *Indiana Historical Collections*, XXIV-XXVI, Indianapolis: Indiana Historical Bureau, 1942.

Severance, Frank H. (ed.), *Millard Fillmore Papers*, 2 vols. *Publications of the Buffalo Historical Society*, X and XI, Buffalo, 1907.

Shanks, Henry Thomas (ed.), *The Papers of Willie Person Mangum*, 5 vols. Raleigh: State Department of Archives and History, 1950-1956.

Slater, Joseph (ed.), *The Correspondence of Emerson and Carlyle.* New York: Columbia University Press, 1964.

Van Tyne, Claude H. (ed.), *The Letters of Daniel Webster from Documents Owned Principally by the New Hampshire Historical Society.* New York: McClure, Phillips and Company, 1902.

Webster, Daniel, "Letter of Daniel Webster, 1833," *American Historical Review*, XXV (1920), 695-697.

## F. MEMOIRS, DIARIES, TRAVEL ACCOUNTS, AND REMINISCENCES

Adams, Charles Francis (ed.), *The Memoirs of John Quincy Adams, Comprising Portions of His Diary from 1795 to 1848*, 12 vols. Philadelphia: J. B. Lippincott and Company, 1874-1877.

Benton, Thomas Hart, *Thirty Years' View: or, A History of the American Government for Thirty Years from 1820-1850*, 2 vols. New York: D. Appleton and Company, 1856.

Bonney, Mrs. Catharina V. R., *A Legacy of Historical Gleanings*, 2 vols. Albany: J. Munsell, 1875.

Clark, G. J. (ed.), *Memoir, Autobiography and Correspondence of Jeremiah Mason.* Kansas City, Missouri: Vernon Law Book Company, 1926.

Fitzpatrick, J. C. (ed.), "Autobiography of Martin Van Buren," *Annual Report of the American Historical Association*, II (1918).

Forney, John W., *Anecdotes of Public Men.* New York: Harper & Brothers, 1873.

Greeley, Horace, *Recollections of a Busy Life.* New York: J. B. Ford & Co., 1868.

Hamilton, James A., *Reminiscences of James A. Hamilton; or Men and Events, At Home and Abroad, During Three Quarters of a Century.* New York: Charles Scribner and Company, 1869.

[Hamilton, Thomas], *Men and Manners in America,* 2 vols. 2nd ed. Philadelphia: Carey, Lea and Blanchard, 1833.

Harvey, Peter, *Reminiscences and Anecdotes of Daniel Webster.* Boston: Little, Brown and Company, 1877.

Hildreth, Richard, *My Connection with the Atlas Newspaper.* Boston: Whipple and Damrell, 1839.

Lawrence, William R. (ed.), *Extracts from the Diary and Correspondence of the Late Amos Lawrence with a Brief Account of Some Incidents in His Life.* Boston: Gould and Lincoln, 1855.

Martineau, Harriet, *A Retrospect of Western Travel,* 2 vols. London: Saunders and Otley, 1838.

McClure, Alexander K., *Old Time Notes of Pennsylvania,* 2 vols. Philadelphia: John C. Winston Company, 1905.

Parker, Edward G., *Reminiscences of Rufus Choate, The Great American Advocate.* New York: Mason Brothers, 1860.

Perry, Benjamin F., *Reminiscences of Public Men.* Philadelphia: J. D. Avil & Co., 1883.

Poore, Ben: Perley, *Perley's Reminiscences of Sixty Years in the National Metropolis,* 2 vols. Philadelphia: Hubbard Brothers, 1886.

Seward, Frederick W. (ed.), *William H. Seward: An Autobiography from 1801 to 1834. With a Memoir of His Life, and Selections from His Letters, 1831-1846.* New York: Derby and Miller, 1891.

Smith, Oliver H., *Early Indiana Trials and Sketches. Reminiscences of Hon. O. H. Smith.* Cincinnati: Moore, Wilstach, Keys & Co., Printers, 1858.

[Smith, Seba], *My Thirty Years Out of the Senate, By Major Jack Downing.* New York: Oaksmith and Company, 1859.

Tuckerman, Bayard (ed.), *The Diary of Philip Hone, 1828-1851,* 2 vols. New York: Dodd, Mead and Company, 1889.

Weed, Harriet A. (ed.), *Autobiography of Thurlow Weed.* Boston: Houghton, Mifflin and Company, 1884.

Winthrop, Robert C., Jr., *A Memoir of Robert C. Winthrop.* Boston: Little, Brown and Company, 1897.

# II. SECONDARY WORKS

## A. MONOGRAPHS AND SPECIAL STUDIES

Baxter, Maurice G., *Daniel Webster & The Supreme Court*. Amherst: University of Massachusetts Press, 1966.

Blakeslee, George Hubbard, "The History of the Antimasonic Party," 2 vols. Unpublished doctoral dissertation, Harvard University, 1903.

Brauer, Kinley J., *Cotton versus Conscience: Massachusetts Whig Politics and Southwestern Expansion, 1843-1848* Lexington: University of Kentucky Press, 1967.

Buley, R. Carlyle, *The Old Northwest: Pioneer Period, 1815-1840*, 2 vols. Indianapolis: Indiana Historical Society, 1950.

Burnham, Walter Dean, *Presidential Ballots, 1836-1892*. Baltimore: Johns Hopkins Press, 1955.

Bowers, Claude G., *The Party Battles of the Jackson Period*. Boston: Houghton Mifflin Company, 1922.

Carroll, Eber Malcolm, *Origins of the Whig Party*. Durham: Duke University Press, 1925.

Catterall, Ralph C. H., *The Second Bank of the United States*. Chicago: University of Chicago Press, 1903.

Darling, Arthur B., *Political Changes in Massachusetts, 1824-1848*. New Haven: Yale University Press, 1925.

Eaton, Clement, *Henry Clay and the Art of American Politics*. Boston: Little, Brown and Company, 1957.

Freehling, William W., *Prelude to Civil War: The Nullification Controversy in South Carolina, 1816-1836*. New York: Harper & Row, 1966.

Livermore, Shaw, Jr., *The Twilight of Federalism: The Disintegration of the Federalist Party, 1815-1830*. Princeton: Princeton University Press, 1962.

Lynch, William O., *Fifty Years of Party Warfare, 1789-1837*. Indianapolis: Bobbs-Merrill Company, 1931.

McCormick, Richard P., *The Second American Party System: Party Formation in the Jacksonian Era*. Chapel Hill: University of North Carolina Press, 1966.

Mering, John Vollmer, *The Whig Party in Missouri*. Columbia: University of Missouri Press, 1967.

Mueller, Henry R., *The Whig Party in Pennsylvania*. New York, 1922.

Reed, John Julius, "The Emergence of the Whig Party in the North: Massachusetts, New York, Pennsylvania, and Ohio." Unpublished doctoral dissertation, University of Pennsylvania, 1953.

Remini, Robert V., *Andrew Jackson and the Bank War*. New York: W. W. Norton & Company, Inc., 1967.

Schlesinger, Arthur M., Jr., *The Age of Jackson*. Boston: Little, Brown and Company, 1946.

Snyder, Charles McCool, *The Jacksonian Heritage: Pennsylvania Politics, 1833-1848*. Harrisburg: Pennsylvania Historical and Museum Commission, 1958.

Stanwood, Edward, *A History of the Presidency from 1788 to 1897*. New ed. Boston: Houghton Mifflin Company, 1928.

Thompson, Charles Manfred, *The Illinois Whigs Before 1846. University of Illinois Studies in the Social Sciences*, vol. IV. Urbana: University of Illinois, 1915.

Van Deusen, Glyndon G., *The Jacksonian Era, 1828-1848*. New York: Harper and Brothers, 1959.

Weisenburger, Francis P., *The Passing of the Frontier, 1825-1850*, vol. III of *The History of the State of Ohio*, 6 vols. Edited by Carl Wittke. Columbus: Ohio State Archaeological and Historical Society, 1941.

## B. BIOGRAPHIES

Barnes, Thurlow Weed, *Memoir of Thurlow Weed*. Boston: Houghton Mifflin and Company, 1884.

Benson, Allan L., *Daniel Webster*. New York: Cosmopolitan Book Corporation, 1929.

Binney, Charles C., *The Life of Horace Binney*. Philadelphia: J. B. Lippincott Company, 1903.

Capers, Gerald M., *John C. Calhoun-Opportunist: A Reappraisal*. Gainesville: University of Florida Press, 1960.

Carson, James Petigru, *Life, Letters and Speeches of James Louis Petigru: The Union Man of South Carolina*. Washington: W. H. Lowdermilk and Company, 1920.

Cleves, Freeman, *Old Tippecanoe: William Henry Harrison and His Time*. New York: Charles Scribner's Sons, 1939.

Coleman, Mrs. Chapman (ed.), *The Life of John J. Crittenden, With Selections from His Correspondence and Speeches*, 2 vols. Philadelphia: J. B. Lippincott and Company, 1871.

Current, Richard N., *Daniel Webster and the Rise of National Conservatism*. Boston: Little, Brown and Company, 1955.

Curtis, George Ticknor, *Life of James Buchanan, Fifteenth President of the United States*, 2 vols. New York: Harper and Brothers, 1883.

—————, *Life of Daniel Webster*, 2 vols. 5th ed. New York: D. Appleton and Company, 1893.

Duberman, Martin B., *Charles Francis Adams, 1807-1886.* Boston: Houghton Mifflin Company, 1961.

Emerson, Donald E., *Richard Hildreth. Johns Hopkins University Studies in Historical and Political Science,* Ser. LXIV, No. 2. Baltimore: Johns Hopkins Press, 1946.

Frothingham, Paul Revere, *Edward Everett, Orator and Statesman.* Boston: Houghton Mifflin Company, 1925.

Fuess, Claude M., *Rufus Choate: The Wizard of the Law.* New York: Minton, Balch & Company, 1928.

—————, *The Life of Caleb Cushing,* 2 vols. New York: D. Appleton and Company, 1923.

—————, *Daniel Webster,* 2 vols. Boston: Little, Brown and Company, 1930.

Goebel, Dorothy Burne, *William Henry Harrison, a Political Biography. Indiana Historical Collections,* XXV. Indianapolis: Historical Bureau of the Indiana Library, 1926.

Gordon, Armistead C., *William Fitzhugh Gordon, A Virginian of the Old School: His Life, Times and Contemporaries, 1787-1858.* New York: Neale Publishing Company, 1909.

Govan, Thomas Payne, *Nicholas Biddle, Nationalist and Public Banker, 1786-1844.* Chicago: University of Chicago Press, 1959.

Hatcher, William B., *Edward Livingston: Jeffersonian Republican and Jacksonian Democrat.* Baton Rouge: Louisiana State University Press, 1940.

Howe, Mark Antony DeWolfe, *Life and Letters of George Bancroft,* 2 vols. New York: Charles Scribners Sons, 1908.

Hunt, Louise Livingston, *Memoir of Mrs. Edward Livingston: With Letters Hitherto Unpublished.* New York: Harper & Brothers, 1886.

Korngold, Ralph, *Thaddeus Stevens: A Being Darkly Wise and Rudely Great.* New York: Harcourt, Brace and Company, 1955.

Lanman, Charles, *The Private Life of Daniel Webster.* New York: Harper & Brothers, 1852.

Lodge, Henry Cabot, *Daniel Webster.* New York: Houghton, Mifflin and Company, 1884.

March, Charles W., *Daniel Webster and His Contemporaries.* 4th ed. New York: Charles Scribner, 1859.

Meigs, William M., *The Life of John Caldwell Calhoun,* 2 vols. New York: Neale Publishing Company, 1917.

Morison, Samuel Eliot, *The Life and Letters of Harrison Gray Otis, Federalist, 1765-1848,* 2 vols. Boston: Houghton Mifflin Company, 1913.

Ogg, Frederic Austin, *Daniel Webster*. Philadelphia: George W. Jacobs and Company, 1914.

Parks, Joseph Howard, *John Bell of Tennseess*. Baton Rouge: Louisiana State University Press, 1950.

Parton, James, *Life of Andrew Jackson,* 3 vols. New York: Mason Brothers, 1861.

Richardson, Charles Francis and Elizabeth Miner (Thomas) Richardson, *Charles Miner, a Pennsylvania Pioneer*. Wilkes-Barre: n.p., 1916.

Scott, Nancy N. (ed.), *A Memoir of Hugh Lawson White, Judge of the Supreme Court of Tennessee, Member of the Senate of the Senate of the United States, etc. With Selections from His Speeches and Correspondence*. Philadelphia: J. B. Lippincott and Company, 1856.

Story, William W. (ed.), *Life and Letters of Joseph Story,* 2 vols. Boston: Charles C. Little and James Brown, 1851.

Tyler, Lyon Gardiner, *The Letters and Times of the Tylers,* 2 vols. Richmond: Whittet and Shepperson, 1884.

Van Deusen, Glyndon G., *The Life of Henry Clay*. Boston: Little, Brown and Company, 1937.

————, *Thurlow Weed: Wizard of the Lobby*. Boston: Little, Brown and Company, 1947.

Warden, Robert B., *An Account of the Private Life and Public Services of Salmon Portland Chase*. Cincinnati: Wilstach, Baldwin and Company, 1874.

Weisenburger, Francis P., *The Life of John McLean: A Politician on the United States Supreme Court*. Columbus: Ohio State University Press, 1937.

Wiltse, Charles Maurice, *John C. Calhoun,* 3 vols. Indianapolis: Bobbs-Merrill Company, 1944-1951.

Woodley, Thomas Frederick, *Thaddeus Stevens*. Harrisburg: Telegraph Press, 1934.

## C. PERIODICAL ARTICLES

Andrews, J. Cutler, "The Antimasonic Movement in Western Pennsylvania," *Western Pennsylvania Historical Magazine*, XVIII (1935), 255-266.

C [sic], "Whig and Tory," *New England Magazine*, VII (1834), 234-238.

Current, Richard N., "Love, Hate, and Thaddeus Stevens," *Pennsylvania History*, XIV (1947), 259-272.

Darling, Arthur B., "The Workingmen's Party in Massachusetts, 1833-
    1834," *American Historical Review*, XXIX (1923), 81-86.
————, "Jacksonian Democracy in Massachusetts, 1824-1848,"
    *American Historical Review*, XXIX (1924), 271-287.
Denny, Harmar, "Anti-Masonic Days Recalled," *Lancaster County
    Historical Society Papers*, XV (1911), 225-229.
Ferguson, Russell J. (ed.), "Minutes of the Young Men's Whig As-
    sociation of Pittsburgh, 1834," *Western Pennsylvania Historical
    Magazine*, XIX (1936), 213-220.
Fox, Dixon Ryan, "The Economic Status of the New York Whigs,"
    *Political Science Quarterly*, XXXIII (1918), 501-518.
Gresham, Lunia Paul, "The Public Career of Hugh Lawson White,"
    *Tennessee Historical Quarterly*, III (1944), 291-318.
Marshall, Lynn L., "The Strange Stillbirth of the Whig Party," *Amer-
    ican Historical Review*, LXXII (1967), 445-468.
Moore, Powell, "The Revolt Against Jackson in Tennessee, 1835-
    1836," *Journal of Southern History*, II (1936), 335-359.
Parish, Peter J., "Daniel Webster, New England, and the West," *Jour-
    nal of American History*, LIV (1967), 524-549.
Pessen, Edward, "Did Labor Support Jackson?: The Boston Story,"
    *Political Science Quarterly*, LXIV (1949), 262-274.
Prichett, John Perry (ed.), " 'Friends' of the Constitution, 1836,"
    *New England Quarterly*, IX (1936), 679-683.
Roberts, Solomon W., "Reminiscences of the First Railroad Over the
    Allegheny Mountain," *Pennsylvania Magazine of History and
    Biography*, II (1878), 370-393.
Sellers, Charles Grier, Jr., "Who Were the Southern Whigs?" *American
    Historical Review*, LIX (1954), 335-346.
Silsbee, Nathaniel, "Biographical Notes," Essex Institute *Historical
    Collections*, XXXV (1899), 1-79.
[Ticknor, George], "Speeches and Forensic Arguments, by Daniel
    Webster," *American Quarterly Review*, IX (1831), 420-457.
Wade, J. D., "The Authorship of David Crockett's 'Autobiography,' "
    *Georgia Historical Quarterly*, IV (1922), 265-268.
Williamson, Joseph, "Daniel Webster's Visit to Maine in 1835," *His-
    torical Magazine*, XIX (1871), 11-13.
Worner, William Frederic, "Daniel Webster in Lancaster; Observance
    of His Death," *Lancaster County Historical Society Papers*,
    XXVIII (1924), 118-120.

# INDEX

Adams, Charles Francis: on weakness of the National Republican party, 69; on dissolution of Masonry in Massachusetts, 81; on selfish ambitions of Webster, Everett, and Davis, 95-96; on Webster's nomination in Massachusetts, 108n82; encourages Hallett, 131; on Webster's defeat in Pennsylvania, 144; works to prevent Webster-Antimasonic alliance, 145-146

Adams, John Quincy: on Webster appointment to London, 3; on Jackson's Harvard degree, 45-46; on break-up of parties, 69; Antimasonic candidate for governor of Massachusetts (1833), 77-78; works to bring National Republicans and Antimasons together, 78-79; refuses further aid, 79-80; advises Antimasons to support Davis, 81; defeated for the United States Senate, 95; notes Armstrong's dissatisfaction, 96-97; on Whig defeats in Connecticut and Rhode Island, 99; on S. S. Southworth, 100; declines to give opinion on Harrison's Antimasonry, 142; on election of 1836, 158, 159; mentioned, 4, 8, 70-73 *passim*, 82, 83, 131-132, 155, 156

Address of the Antimasonic seceders in Pennsylvania, 141-142

"Address to the Antimasonic Republicans of the Commonwealth of Massachusetts," 155

Albany *Argus*: denies Webster-Van Buren "grand league," 32, 44; on Webster's expense account, 107n58

Albany Regency, 32, 64

Allen, Samuel C., 78, 82

Antimasonic party: origins, 14n30; and election of 1832, 8-12 *passim*; decline, 69; in Massachusetts, 77; in Pennsylvania, 126-128

Appleton, Nathan, 64, 76

Armstrong, Samuel F., 96-97

Ayres, William: requests Harrison's views on Masonry, 138

Bailache, John: on Webster's candidacy, 112; mentioned, 103

Bailey, John, 81-82

Bancroft, George, 83, 159

Bank of the United States: in the election of 1832, 11; mentioned *passim*

Barbour, James: on Whig strategy in election of 1836, 124

Barbour, Philip P.: on Webster in the House of Representatives, 4

Barry, William: on Webster's visit to Cincinnati, 42

Bates, Isaac, 96

Bates, William: conversation with Webster, 1

Bell, John, 88